LOOK WHO'S TALKING ABOUT: *On My Honor, I Will*

"Values such as integrity, honesty, good faith dealing, and respect are the foundation for long-term success. That's what *On My Honor, I Will* is all about."
> —Ken Blanchard, Ph.D., author of *The One Minute Manager*

"A provocative approach to untangling and demystifying the thorny issues of ethical management in uncertain and murky times."
> —Ron Zemke, co-author of *Service America: Doing Business in the New Economy*

"I enthusiastically endorse *On My Honor* for one very simple reason: These gentlemen are espousing principles that work—that worked yesterday, work today and will work tomorrow, perhaps even better."
> —Zig Ziglar, author of *See You at the Top*

"Shows how straightforward honor and ethics can help build a successful business."
> —*Seattle Times*

"A straight shooting book."
> —*Success* magazine

"*On My Honor* is bursting with down-to-earth stories and reflections on the importance of strong moral character in the practice of business."

—Gary E. Edwards, President, Ethics Resource Center, Inc.

"Will help us…breed success in our business, our community, and personal lives."

—Edwin M. Cooperman, Chairman and co-CEO, American Express Travel Related Services Co., Inc.

"*On My Honor* is just the prescription for our rapidly declining moral values. Pennington and Bockmon have done yeoman's work to make their case."

—Walter Williams, Distinguished Professor of Economics at George Mason University and syndicated newspaper columnist

"*On My Honor* may help many troubled decision makers rethink and apply to their work and their companies the simple morality they learned as children."

—Robert L. Dilenschneider, author of *Power and Influence*

"While people 'scout for answers,' this book provides a refresher course on values/behaviors desperately needed in today's business world."

—Susan RoAne, author of *How to Work a Room*

ON MY HONOR, I WILL

Leading With Integrity In Changing Times

Randy Pennington and Marc Bockmon
Foreword by Zig Ziglar

Treasure House
An Imprint of Destiny Image Publishers, Inc.®

Treasure House

An Imprint of
Destiny Image Publishers, Inc.®
P.O. Box 310
Shippensburg, PA 17257-0310
ISBN 1-56043-846-0

Printed in the United States of America for Worldwide Distribution.

Library of Congress Cataloging in Publication Data

Pennington, Randy
On my honor, I will: leading with integrity in changing
times
1. Success—Psychological aspects.   2. Success in business.
3. Leadership—moral and ethical aspects.
I. Bockmon, Marc, 1943-   . II. Title

Inside the U.S., call toll free to order:
1-800-722-6774

To Mary, my partner in love and life.
Randy Pennington

*To Marie, the woman of integrity who
became my wife.*
Marc Bockmon

ACKNOWLEDGMENTS

Every effort to expand knowledge, encourage thinking, and influence behavior is a shared process. This project is no exception. We wish to say "thank you" to the following people and organizations for their assistance and encouragement. Without them, this project would not have been as enjoyable or successful.

- William C. Gamble of the Boy Scouts of America Circle Ten Council for his support and ability to get things done.
- Ray Robbins, Roger Staubach, John P. Hayes, and Zig Ziglar for giving their support early in the project and continuing it to the end.
- Steve Ventura for helping us brainstorm many of our original ideas.
- The corporate public relations professionals and executive assistants who helped us get to the right people and receive the right information.
- Howard Putnam for providing a living example of high integrity, leadership, and professionalism to work toward.

- Dennis & Niki McCuisiton, Al Walker, Jim Cathcart, Mark Sanborn, Susan RoAne, Nido Qubein, Jim & Naomi Rhode, Glenna Salsbury, Lou Heckler, and Bob & Jane Handly who have given encouragement, ideas for improvement, and friendship.
- The individuals and organizations discussed in this book, providing endorsements and using the principles of honor and integrity to succeed. You are the true leaders.

PREFACE TO THE REVISED EDITION

One of cartoonist Gary Larson's classic Far Side comics shows a dinosaur behind a podium speaking to a group of his peers. The caption reads, "The picture is pretty bleak gentlemen. The world's climates are changing, the mammals are taking over, and we all have a brain about the size of a walnut." There are many who believe that to be an accurate description of our society, organizations, and leaders in today's changing times. James Patterson and Peter Kim provide a snapshot of our nation's views on leadership in their book *The Second American Revolution.*[1] According to their research, "two in three Americans don't believe we have any leaders with the ability to address the nation's ills; half of Americans don't have anyone in their family they'd like to model themselves after; and seventy percent of Americans believe our nation doesn't have heroes anymore."

We became concerned about the lack of trust in our leaders in 1989. *On My Honor, I Will* began as an effort to

---

[1] James Petterson and Peter Kim, *The Second American Revolution* (William Morrow, 1994) 26.

bring a sense of integrity back into the work place and society as a whole. A daily review of the headlines proves that we have a long way to go to achieve our goal.

Since its first publication in 1992, we have continued our growth in this area and learned from wonderful people throughout the world. Many are clients who have applied these concepts to their organizations. Others are people who read the original publication and cared enough to share their thoughts and ideas. The result is an updated work that reflects much of our current thinking in the following areas:

- **Everything is connected.** Successful organizations are built by successful people, and it is difficult to maintain long-term excellence in one area of life when the remaining parts are not in harmony. We now see life at work and life away from work more closely intertwined than at any time in our history. Effective leaders understand the importance of those relationships.

- **Organizations are more than just the places we work.** Families, civic groups, and communities face similar issues and show the same tendencies as businesses, proving the adage "there is no new truth." The principles that create successful companies can be adapted to create successful families, neighborhoods, and countries.

- **Natural laws affect more than most of us ever imagine**. Hyrum Smith defines natural laws as "fundamental patterns of nature and life that human experience and testing have shown to be valid."[2] We recognize them as self-evident truths that govern our

---

[2] Hyrum W. Smith, *The 10 Natural Laws of Successful Time and Life Management* (Warner Books, 1994) 12.

behavior and relationships. Natural laws are not part of any single belief system, although they are incorporated in many. We both operate from a Judeo-Christian ethic, but the principles can be found in the teachings of great thinkers from all cultures.

- **Everyone is a leader.** Each of us has the potential for leadership in at least one area—we each have the responsibility for leading our own lives. However, most of us have opportunities for leadership in a number of areas. Families, relationships, civic groups, churches and synagogues, youth development activities, schools and community groups all depend on leaders who build trust, loyalty, and commitment.

- **Developing leaders for the future is our most important challenge.** A recent study of 3,000 undergraduate business students from 31 universities reported that 95% admitted cheating during high school and college. Although only 1% to 2% reported cheating on a regular basis, the students in the survey see themselves as less ethical than their parents.[3] The hectic pace that drives each of our lives often causes us to lose sight of anything beyond today. But to be responsible leaders today, we must develop responsible leadership for tomorrow.

---

[3] Lee Berton, "Business Students Hope To Cheat And Prosper, A New Study Shows," *The Wall Street Journal*, April 25, 1995.

We hope you will enjoy this edition of *On My Honor, I Will*. It has been recast as more of a leadership book than a business book, but the overall message remains the same. Long-term success depends on our ability to honor ourselves and others through integrity and personal performance.

Randy Pennington & Marc Bockmon
May 1995

How to Use This Book as a Learning Tool

This book is a quick and easy read. You should be able to complete it in a relatively short period of time. The value, however, comes from completing the exercises that appear within and at the end of each chapter. That is why we recommend that you read the book at least twice to gain the maximum benefit. You should read it the first time to focus on the main theme and concepts. Read it a second time to complete and think about the exercises and their application to your life and organization.

On My Honor, I Will can also serve as a guide for personal and/or organizational development. If you choose to use it in that way, we suggest the following:

- identify specific areas for action and improvement based on your responses to the exercises at the end of the book
- focus on one area of mastery at a time rather than working on all the concepts at once
- set detailed goals for improvement, making sure to include specific results you expect
- track your performance and look for feedback from others
- spend time evaluating yourself and refining your performance

We gain new understanding and perspective every time we read this book…and we know what is in it. Go back to the lessons shared here and explore them often. If you are like us, you will learn something new each time. Happy learning and growing!

THE SCOUT OATH

On my honor I will do my best:
1. To do my duty to God and my country, and to obey the Scout Law;
2. To help other people at all times;
3. To keep myself physically strong, mentally awake, and morally straight.

"The central need of our times is to find the road we lost or abandoned, and to recover the values we have rejected in favor of every man for himself in pursuit of egoistic goals."

—Laslo Nagy
Secretary-General World Organization of the Scout Movement

CONTENTS

Foreword xxi

Chapter 1 Once Upon a Business Trip 1

Chapter 2 On My Honor, I Will 11

Chapter 3 Do My Best 29

Chapter 4 To Do My Duty 49

Chapter 5 To God and My Country 71

Chapter 6 To Obey the Scout Law 87

Chapter 7 To Help Other People at All Times 115

Chapter 8 To Keep Myself Physically Strong, Mentally Awake, and Morally Straight 141

Chapter 9 Living the Oath—Life Style Integrity 153

Chapter Notes 177

FOREWORD

There's a persistent belief that "nice guys finish last." Not only do they not finish last, but they ultimately finish at, or near the top, while the "bad guys" consistently finish behind the eight-ball, behind bars, or near the bottom. *On My Honor* by Randy Pennington and Marc Bockmon gives some magnificent insights and instructions that will help make you a winner in your personal, family, and business life. Here is an on-target, up-to-date, common-sense approach to why we must be teaching principles, procedures, and values that worked in the beginning of our country's history and will work even better today.

In this day and age many facets of our society are coming apart at the seams, it's refreshing and exciting to read a book based on the principles taught in the Boy Scout organization. In this day of drive-by shootings, X-rated "entertainment," and drug and alcohol problems, teenage pregnancies, crime, theft and violence, it's refreshing to have authors who boldly advocate the principles of pledging, "On my honor, I will do my best." When we adopt the principles of "honor and best effort," we're building a solid foundation for success. When we include courtesy, kindness, obedience, cheerfulness, and friendliness, we describe an individual who will be a success in his personal, business, social, and family life.

When a Scout (or you) pledges to do his duty to God and country and to keep himself morally straight and physically clean, he moves out of the crowd at the bottom and starts climbing toward the top. When a person agrees to be trustworthy, think of what that means in a society where, according to a recent best-seller, 91 percent of the people in America will indiscriminately lie about a host of things.

What's exciting about the principles espoused in *On My Honor* is the fact that they work in every facet of our lives. Question: Did you ever wonder why in the 1770s three million Americans produced Thomas Jefferson, Benjamin Franklin, George Washington, John Adams, James Monroe, James Madison, and a host of other truly brilliant leaders, and in 1990 250 million Americans produced _____? (I believe you would be hard-pressed to find even one name you would be willing to list as having the greatness of the men listed above.)

Could it be that what those early Americans were taught had a direct bearing on their performance and accomplishments? For example, according to the Thomas Jefferson Research Institute, in the 1770s over 90 percent of our educational thrust was aimed at teaching moral values. At that time, most of the education was handled in the home, church, or church-supported schools. By 1926 the percentage of moral training had reduced to 6 percent, and by 1951 the percentage was so low you could not even measure it.

Now tie this to the fact that according to a May 1989, issues of *Psychology Today*, reporting on a study of 1,139 chief executive officers who had an average salary of $356,000, their number-one asset was their integrity and their number-one priority was their family. Now combine this with the April 28, 1986, issue of *Fortune* magazine, where we learn that 91 percent of CEOs of the Fortune 500 companies are people of faith, which means they probably received their moral and values training at home, or in a house of worship. In short, the truly successful people in all areas of their lives build their careers on a solid ethical base.

In this easy-to-read example-filled book, Randy Pennington and Marc Bockmon give example after example right out of today's society of men and women who have achieved remarkable results. I enthusiastically endorse *On My Honor* for one very simple reason: These gentlemen are espousing principles that work—that worked yesterday, work today, and will work tomorrow, perhaps even better. Tom Peters expressed it well when he said integrity always has been and always will be the key to successful accomplishment. You will both enjoy and benefit from *On My Honor*.

—Zig Ziglar

CHAPTER 1

ONCE UPON A BUSINESS TRIP

2:15 p.m.   We were at an impasse. Mr. Horton[1] had hired us to provide consultation services for his firm. The project had gone well, and everyone was pleased. In fact, after the project was begun, Mr. Horton had agreed to extend the scope of the agreement for an extra fee. Now, he was claiming he had always assumed the extra work had been part of the original package and denied agreeing to any additional charges.

We **knew** we were right, and Mr. Horton **said** he was right. The old saying, "An unwritten agreement isn't worth the paper it's written on," came to mind. Obviously, without written evidence or corroborating testimony, judgment would default to Horton's firm.

"What about Mike Johnson?"[2] I asked, remembering that Horton's Vice President of Finance had attended the meeting where the extra work was discussed, priced, and approved.

The client gave us a "now-I've-got-you" smile and picked up the phone. He buzzed his superior and asked him to join us. When Mr. Johnson arrived, Horton gave him the details of the dispute, making his own position perfectly clear.

Johnson listened carefully until his associate finished, then shook his head: "Oh, no! They told us about the extra charge up front, and we both agreed it was fair! Don't you remember? In fact, you said the price was more than fair!"

Horton mumbled something, and thanked his supervisor. After Johnson left, Horton began shuffling papers on his desk. There was a somewhat awkward silence, which was broken by my associate who said with relief, "I'm glad Mr. Johnson remembered."

Horton shook his head in disgust, "Yeah, he's a real Boy Scout."

4:00 p.m. As we drove back to the airport, we began to wonder about Horton's disparaging remark that Johnson was a "real Boy Scout." The implication was that anyone who valued integrity more than money was somewhat defective in judgment.

And what about Horton? Had he fallen into the mind trap of believing greed was good? That the end justified the means? That honor and integrity were not consistent with long-term success? That the principle of doing what is right is archaic, outmoded, and fit only for children? If so, a quick scan of recent headlines would have indicated that he was not alone in his belief. It was almost as if there had been a shift in moral values. If this was true, it might explain the apparent moral malaise in American business and society.

We were not the only ones to notice that American leaders and businesses had a problem. A rash of pop-management books have sought to offer quick-fix solutions by concentrating on specific aspects of business. The problem is, these solutions are often more "quick" than a true fix. Besides, quick-fix solutions, like quick-fix diets, usually don't last. It takes time to change your way of eating—or living.

The search for solutions has birthed so many books that one client defined the phenomena as MBBS—"management by best-seller." In our frantic search to find success, we are in danger of becoming a nation of Ponce de Leon's, seeking a magic spring that would restore youthful vitality to our careers, our businesses, and our lives.

It isn't so much that such books aren't helpful—most are. It is just that we can't bring about internal change with external medicine. To genuinely increase our organizational and individual success, the change must come from within. This takes more time and effort, but it brings lasting change. It's the kind of change that shifts the focus from *who* is right to *what* is right. Then and only then can we be truly successful.

4:20 p.m. We arrived at the airport, checked our luggage, and ordered coffee in the terminal's restaurant. My colleague, obviously still bothered by Horton's remark, sighed and asked me what the phrase "a real Boy Scout" meant to me.

"One who lives by the Scout Oath," I replied. "Remember it?"

> **"On my honor, I will do my best:**
> **To do my duty to God and my country, and to obey the**
> **Scout Law.**
> **To help other people at all times,**
> **To keep myself physically strong, mentally awake, and**
> **morally straight."**

Somewhat to the amazement of the waitress, arriving with our coffee, we recited the Scout Oath together.

We moved on to recite the Scout Law:

> **"A scout is trustworthy, loyal, helpful, friendly,**
> **courteous, kind,**
> **obedient, cheerful, thrifty, brave, clean, and reverent."**

The waitress departed with a puzzled look on her face. My friend remarked, "These are admirable qualities. Why did Horton use the term 'Boy Scout' as if it were a derogatory term? Isn't it a compliment? Wouldn't we want 'Boy Scouts' and 'Girl Scouts' for employees? For customers? For suppliers? For supervisors, managers, and leaders?"

I had to admit these were good questions, and the answers seemed obvious. After all, it was the Scout Oath and the Scout Law that first caused business people to devote their time, talents, and financial resources to the movement. These early Scouting pioneers recognized that the virtues that made good scouts also made good citizens, good customers, good competitors, good employees, and good leaders.

Consequently, it's not surprising that Scouting is best known for character building and leadership development. Character building was a major goal of the Scouting movement from the beginning, back in 1907 when retired British General Sir Robert Baden-Powell, a war hero who had achieved national prominence, organized a camp for twenty boys. A year later, he published his first Boy Scout manual, and the movement swept England. In his book, *Scouting for Boys*, Baden-Powell proclaimed, "Scouting is a school of citizenship...."

The strong emphasis on the outdoors and citizenship soon endeared Scouts and Scouting to both boys and adults across England. In 1909, American businessman William Boyce was visiting England and became lost in the famous London fog. A Boy Scout found him and, practicing the Scout Habit ("Do a good turn daily"), guided him back to his hotel. Impressed, Boyce was determined to bring the movement to America. The following year, he succeeded. On May 6, 1911, the Boy Scouts of America developed their own Oath along the model of their British brethren.

Virtually nothing in America is the way it was in 1911, yet through decades that brought boom and bust, recession and depression, wars and rumors of war, changes in transportation, communication, and life styles, the Scout Oath and the Scout Law have remained unchanged. They are intact for the same reason the Bill of Rights and other self-evident truths remain intact—because they work. Nevertheless, our client had spoken disparagingly of the virtues of being a "Boy Scout." Why? Had he too been "lost in the fog" thinking he should be applauded for acting unfairly to save the company money?

5:20 p.m. I absently creased my napkin into neat accordion-like folds, while memories of my Scouting days flooded my mind. "It was a simpler world back when we were Boy Scouts," I said.

"Sure it was," my colleague replied. "We were pledged to keep the Scout Oath and obey the Scout Law. Sure, it was idealistic, but what's wrong with that? It's better to try to reach those kinds of goals and fail than not even try at all. Life would be simpler and better if everyone behaved like a 'real Boy Scout'."

"Yes, it would," I replied. "It would work for organizations and their leaders just like it works for youth. It's the epitome of 'honesty is the best policy,' 'the customer is always right,' 'going the extra mile,' 'lending a helping hand,' and all of that. It's the Golden Rule expounded and explained."

My companion sipped his coffee and thoughtfully replaced the cup in the saucer. "I read an article in *Fortune* magazine some time back that said young workaholics are finding that family and volunteerism are becoming important again," he said. "They're learning you have to sow as well as reap to live a successful life or operate a successful business."

"The Book of Proverbs says, 'As a man thinks, so he is.'[3] If we keep thinking about the Boy Scout Oath and begin to believe it, pretty soon we'd behave it as well. Imagine the impact of a nation of "Business Scouts"! Imagine business people and employees who pledged to be trustworthy, loyal, helpful, friendly, courteous, kind, obedient, cheerful, thrifty, brave, clean, and reverent! Many businesses already operate by these values. If we all did, we just might regain our competitive advantage and be able to work together more collaboratively and successfully."

"Would people do it?" I asked.

"They used to. People once helped each other build homes and raise barns. There was a time when an honest man could borrow money at the bank on a handshake. The beauty of the Scout Oath and Law is that they're like gravity—they work whether you believe in them or not—whether you want it to be that way or not! A scout is trustworthy, right? That's just another word for honesty. We grew up hearing, 'honesty is the best policy.' Why? Because it's the only policy that works to build long-term trust. Oh, you can get away with being dishonest for awhile—but in the end you lose the trust and respect of others that is necessary for success in today's interdependent world. To paraphrase an adage, 'Time eventually wounds all heels!' "

"What would happen if the Scout Oath were applied to American business?" I wondered, my mind whirling with possibilities. "It would change the way we do business from the inside out—not just the outside in! I think a lot of the best-selling business books have missed the need for internal change."

"Applying an external solution to an internal problem is like taking morphine for cancer. It may disguise the symptoms, but it doesn't do anything about the disease."

I nodded. "In fact, easing the pain can make it worse—because it can lull you into a false sense of security, a feeling that all is well when, in fact, all is wrong. It seems to me, a lot of people are trying to be successful while being untrustworthy, disloyal, unhelpful, unfriendly, discourteous, unkind, disobedient, uncheerful, unthrifty, unbrave, unclean, and irreverent," I said.

My associate thought a moment, before observing that many people operate on those premises. Executives and evangelists have been punished for playing fast and loose with the money of others. Stockbrokers have been found guilty of insider trading. Executives at Beechnut, a large baby food company, were found guilty of selling phony apple juice. Several companies were indicted for selling adulterated orange juice, and a major supermarket chain sold it, apparently in full knowledge that it wasn't pure, because they got such a good buy.

In February, 1990, Bolar Pharmaceutical Company was forced by the FDA to remove from the market the largest-selling generic drug in America, a blood pressure medication taken by 500,000 people, because it was discovered the company switched test samples to get the drug approved. Earlier, in October, 1989, Bolar had been forced to pull a generic antibiotic amid similar charges. These two drugs were taken by hundreds of thousands of people and accounted for 47 percent of the company's total sales. Executives had apparently decided to play fast and loose with the health of their customers.

When Watergate conspirator Jeb Stuart McGruder was asked how he had sunk to such a despicable level, he hung his head and said, "I don't know. I guess I just lost my moral compass." Is the real or perceived loss of moral compass the reason for the high level of distrust between management and labor? Could that be the explanation for the erosion of confidence in American products and preachers and politicians?

Whatever the cause, our work in the field of leadership and organizational development convinced my associate and I that both management and employees are feeling a sense of frustration in their relationships. Lack of trust is common. Commitment to companies or customers has become an uncommon commodity.

Today's organizations continually strive to improve every aspect of their operation. However, these efforts often meet with limited success for one specific reason—a lack of trust that destroys relationships and prevents people from working together to improve their situation. The same can be said of governments, schools, religious institutions, and families.

"Somebody ought to write a book about it," I said to my colleague. "It would demonstrate how traditional values provide an organization with a foundation that can stand the test of time."

6:10 p.m. They announced our flight. We paid our check and boarded the plane, thinking about how the principles embodied in the Scout Oath and Law could work to the advantage of organizations and individuals everywhere.

The story you have just read is true, masked sufficiently to disguise the identity of the client and the situation.[4] The more we thought about those of questionable honor referring to those of unquestionable honor as "real Boy Scouts," the more convinced we became that believing and enacting the Boy Scout Oath and Law could favorably impact America and American business.

That's our opinion. You decide for yourself. If, after you've read this book, you conclude the authors are "Boy Scouts"—we will consider that a true compliment.

CHAPTER 2
ON MY HONOR, I WILL

Over sixty years ago, Costin J. Harrell wrote a devotional book[1] that was destined to become a classic. In this book, he related a story told him by Dr. W.F. Tillet of Vanderbilt University about ermine hunting in Europe. Dr. Tillet said the ermine honors his beautiful white coat to such an extent that it leads to his capture. When hunters find an ermine den, they daub the entrance with filth and loose the dogs. When the dogs get hot on the trail, the ermine runs for his den. However, when he arrives and finds he must soil his coat to enter, he turns to face the dogs and fights for his life. The ermine can be captured because he would rather have his coat stained with blood than have it dirtied with filth. Honor is dearer than life!

Death Before Dishonor

Swashbuckling movies have always been popular. When honorable opponents were dueling with swords and one obtained the upper hand, he would ask his defeated foe, "Death or dishonor?" Everyone but the villain always chose death. Even in the land of make-believe, honor was dearer than life.

Few today would hold honor dearer than life. Many would not hold honor dearer than financial gain. Others would even sacrifice honor on the altar of expedience.

Perhaps our ambiguity toward honor is rooted in ignorance. Honor is one of those words we all think we understand—until we're asked to provide the definition. What about you? Do you know what *honor* means? Think about it a moment before you read on.

If you had difficulty describing honor, you are not alone! The point we're trying to make is that it is difficult to live up to an ill-defined standard. The dictionary also takes a couple of trips around the block to define honor.

> **honor 1 a:** good name or public esteem:
> **REPUTATION b:** showing of usu. merited
> respect: **RECOGNITION 2: PRIVILEGE 3:** a
> person of superior standing—now used as a title
> for a holder of high office **4:** one whose worth
> brings respect or fame...**7: CHASTITY,
> PURITY 8 a:** a keen sense of ethical conduct:
> **INTEGRITY b:** one's word given as a
> guarantee of performance.[2]

The definitions continue, but it is interesting that the kind of honor we are discussing doesn't appear until the eighth definition! Since we find honor mentioned so often in the writings of our national patriarchs, we went back to the first American Dictionary, published by Noah Webster in 1828 to see how he defined it:

True nobleness of mind; magnanimity; dignified respect for character, springing from probity, principle or moral rectitude; a distinguishing trait in the character of good men.
An assumed appearance of nobleness; scorn of meanness, springing from the fear of reproach, without regard to principle. [3]

Notice how Noah Webster defined genuine honor succinctly and clearly then, immediately, warned against counterfeits. It's true that not everyone who speaks of honor has it. Ralph Waldo Emerson wrote of one guest, "The louder he talked of his honor, the faster we counted our spoons."

We've all heard the expression, "There's honor even among thieves." Is there? In 1973, Bobby Joe Reickenbacker, the infamous "Bandanna Bandit" was sentenced to 320 years in prison for a series of daring bank robberies. Now reformed and released, Bobby Joe counsels teenagers. He says, "My father was a thief, and from the time I was eleven years old, I wanted to be a big-time bandit like he was. I've been a thief and I've been surrounded by thousands of thieves most of my life. My stealing got me into reform school, city jail, county jail, and state and federal prison. I can say without a moment's hesitation that there is no honor among thieves. That's an illusion fostered by social workers and writers. How can there possibly be honor among the dishonorable? We thieves stole from each other in prison, just like we did when we were on the outside."

Bobby Joe is right. If there was "honor among thieves," they wouldn't be thieves. A person either has honor or he doesn't. It isn't honor if you can turn it on and off.

It's impossible to hold two diametrically opposing value systems in our mind for any length of time. When we try to mix honor and dishonor, we create stresses that shatter our consciences and make long-term success more difficult. The result is that the "honor" we tout is not genuine, but false honor, the loud, brassy, hollow kind that causes others to question our motives and count their spoons.

The fact that false honor exists should not make us skeptical. The false never diminishes the value of the original as long as we can distinguish between the two. If anything, fakes only make the original even more valuable and beautiful. When a Scout proclaims, "On my honor, I will," he isn't talking about assumed or artificial honor, he's talking about the genuine article. He is saying he will, based on his "nobleness of mind, magnanimity, dignified respect for character."

"Scout's honor" is the kind of honor Jefferson wrote about in the Declaration of Independence: "We mutually pledge to each other our lives, our fortunes, our sacred honor."

It is what Congress had in mind when it created the Medal of Honor. The medal was conceived to honor a soldier whose own personal sense of honor caused him to "distinguish himself conspicuously by gallantry and intrepidity at the risk of his life, above and beyond the call of duty." It is fitting that the nation's highest award goes to those who hold honor dearer than life.

We've been working on the definition of honor. What is an "honorable person" or an "honorable organization"? We believe the easiest definition is that an honorable person or organization is one that does the "right thing" regardless of whether or not it's the convenient thing, the profitable thing, or the fun thing. Honor is doing what's right regardless of the consequences. Honor is making commitments and keeping them.

Many American businesses and leaders do believe that honor is sacred. Throughout this book you'll find examples of individual leaders and organizations who have made a commitment to honor and integrity. Not surprisingly, these individuals and organizations are typically recognized leaders in their field. These are not supersaints or moral monks. They are ordinary people with an extraordinary commitment to honor, integrity, and doing what's right. We each have the ability to do the same. However, it requires genuine commitment and hard work.

LEADERSHIP IN ACTION: HOWARD PUTNAM

There are some who rationalize their behavior for the sake of expediency or gain. Like the ermine, honor and integrity may cost us our survival. Yet whatever the cost, persons of honor behave honorably. As a result, they retain honor even in a situation that many consider "dishonorable."

For instance, many passengers felt Braniff International Airways did not act honorably during their first bankruptcy. When Braniff recalled planes in flight, leaving passengers out the price of their tickets and stranded, people were irate. While the corporate honor was sullied, most of those who came under attack: agents, flight attendants, pilots, and even President Howard Putnam acted honorably.

Putnam was President of the up and coming regional carrier Southwest Airlines when he was first contacted by Braniff's Board of Directors. He took the job and promised the Board to do his best to rescue the troubled carrier. As soon as he took office, he found that the airline only had a ten day cash reserve. If he stayed in his post, there was only a slight chance he could save the airline. If he left immediately, he could probably get another job and avoid a black mark on his record. Yet he had made a promise on his honor and felt a promise made was a debt unpaid. He decided to stay with Braniff, do what he could to save it, and if he couldn't, ride the plane down along with everyone else.

In retrospect, it was Putnam's honor that partially contributed to the airline's demise. In the waning days of Braniff's fight to continue operation, a reporter asked Putnam if he could guarantee that Braniff would be flying in a year. Putnam, in a sense putting professional death before dishonor, stated no one could guarantee any company's success or failure. When pressed further he stated that he felt good about the company's prospects, but could not its guarantee survival. The newspaper's report that Putnam was unsure of Braniff's survival resulted in further negative publicity. Yet, in the end, honor won out. Not one shareholder filed suit against Braniff or Braniff management during the bankruptcy proceedings. Harvard University now conducts a course entitled "Ethics of a Bankruptcy" based on Putnam's handling of this difficult situation. Putnam has gone on to a successful career as an entrepreneur and currently shares his leadership experience with many of the country's best-managed organizations.

Be True To Yourself

The January 16, 1990 issue of *Parents' Magazine* reported that 78 percent of respondents in a poll expressed a desire to return to "traditional values and old-fashioned morality." We believe this must be done if we are to survive, much less thrive, as a society.

To be people of honor, we must first be honest about our intents and motives. Once we accept personal responsibility for our behavior and start being totally honest with ourselves, we'll find we "cannot be false to any man."

Honor is a learned behavior. Our children, our co-workers, and our employees learn honor from us. They learn more by observation than they do by conversation. Sometimes, they can't hear what we're saying because what we're doing speaks so loudly.

Little people steal little things because they see big people steal big things with impunity. Little people tell little lies because they hear big shots tell big ones. Why shouldn't an employee falsify a test report on a single component when he sees his supervisor sign off on a big one that's defective? Why shouldn't a secretary take home office supplies when she sees her employer overcharge a customer?

We tell our children, "It's not whether you win or lose, but how you play the game." What they often see by our actions, however, is, "It's not how you play the game; whether you win or lose, it's whether you win!"

People of Honor—People of Action

Leaders who earn the respect of others and achieve their goals understand and live by the **honor principle:** *The honors of long-term success follow the consistent honoring of self and others through integrity and personal performance.*

The power of the Scout Oath as a guide for leaders and organizations is grounded in this principle. The phrase "on my honor" is important, but the "juice flows" when we add "I will." Like the positive pole of an electrical charge, the two simple words *I will* provide the behavioral example of honor.

Unfortunately, many have adopted the approach of "on my honor, I will think about it"; or, "on my honor, I'll let others take responsibility for that decision." The Scout Oath is an active affirmation. Honor is the qualifier, but action is required to show our commitment to doing what is right. Scouts try to do a good turn daily. Somehow, the picture wouldn't be right if the Scout on the corner simply pointed the elderly lady in the right direction, then nudged her into the intersection. It is by positive action that we demonstrate honor, and by honoring ourselves and others we are distinguished from those who do not uphold these principles.

People of honor don't look for escape clauses, excuses, or justifications. They're more concerned with *what's* right than with *who's* right. They hold themselves to that standard in everything they do by mastering the concepts of alignment, admiration, and assurance.

We assume no one reading this book has lived a totally honorable life—certainly neither of those writing it have. However, one robin does not make a spring, and one dishonorable deed does not make a dishonorable person. Many mistakes are committed by decent people who, unfortunately, lose sight of what is right amidst a momentary lapse into desperation or weakness. Circumstances convince them that bending the rules is acceptable "just this once." After the first lapse, it becomes easier, and a habit of deceiving ourselves and others becomes developed.

We are what we habitually do. If we are habitually unreliable, undependable, and dishonorable, we become that. On the other hand, if we make commitments and keep them, if our word is our bond regardless of the cost, then we become what we have been behaving, as we become a person of integrity by behaving like a person of integrity.

Honorable people not only do honorable things; they do them with honorable motives. The closer we get to the ideal, the more positively we impact those around us.

Danny White, former quarterback of the National Football League's Dallas Cowboys, was booed by many when he crossed the union picket line to play during the 1987 football strike. Many of his teammates no doubt disagreed with his decision also. But, to White it was a moral question. He said, "It was a moral issue in that I'd signed a contract. No way could I claim mistreatment, underpayment, or discrimination. I signed a contract to play for the Dallas Cowboys. I felt morally obligated to play."[4]

When Congresswoman Jeannette Rankin voted against the United States entering World War II the day after the Japanese bombed Pearl Harbor, her political career ended. Not many Americans agreed with her point of view, but no one doubted her integrity or that she felt honor-bound to do what she thought was right—regardless of the consequences.

Living a life that is grounded in honor doesn't mean that others will always agree with our decisions. Even honorable people have genuine disagreements over a course of action Living the honor principle helps people trust and respect us, and that is more important than the agreement of others in achieving long-term success as leaders.

Corporations of Honor

Acting honorably is often difficult for individuals. Imagine how challenging it must be for organizations. Yet, history is replete with examples of corporate honor and commitment to doing what's right. There aren't enough pages in this book to make an exhaustive list of the companies, much less of the deeds themselves. However, here are a few examples of organizations that do what's right for honorable reasons. You will hear about others throughout the book.

Reader's Digest was the first magazine to drop cigarette advertising, back when the first Surgeon General's warning about smoking and cancer was released. This cost the magazine millions in lost revenue. They did it because they felt committed to preserving their readers' life and health, as well as providing them with reading enjoyment.

IBM has maintained a set of core values, that goes back to the 1930s which has included respect for the individual, customer service, and excellence. IBM has been "ahead of its time" in other ways too. They started job enrichment in the 1920s and a version of "quality circles" in the 1930s. In the 1950s and 60s, they made IBM synonymous with honoring the customer. Despite past achievements, IBM had to reinvent itself in the late 1980s and early 90s.

Honorable values do not insulate us from competitive environments. IBM initially responded to the new industry climate with restructuring layoffs, transfers, early retirements, and liberal severance programs. Their efforts to honor others in the face of adversity led to a strong perception of fairness from those laid off. IBM has continued to change and evolve in the mid–1990s guided by Thomas Watson's core values of respect for the individual, customer service, and excellence.

Soft Sheen Products, Inc., founded by Edward and Bethann Gardner, is the largest minority-owned manufacturing firm in the U.S.A., with sales over $87 million in 1989. But the business goes beyond profits for the Gardner family. Soft Sheen makes a concerted effort to provide jobs for the African-American community, as well as an opportunity to enhance self-esteem through quality products.

Hallmark Cards, Inc., is the world's largest greeting card company, and is widely considered one of the best places in America to work. (Hallmark was listed in *The 100 Best Companies to Work for in America*, Addison-Wesley, 1984). Hallmark is one of the few businesses that has a tradition of full employment without layoffs. In addition, they offer outstanding employee benefits. Most notably, Hallmark honors those individuals who make it successful—the employees. The company offers interest-free loans for emergencies, college loans for education, physical fitness facilities, and covered parking for those working at the Crown Center complex (a great benefit during harsh Kansas winters). Their commitment to quality gives production employees the right to stop the presses if they feel the product does not meet Hallmark's standards. Hallmark understands what all of the leaders and organizations discussed in this book understand—honoring self and others through integrity and performance are the only way to assure lasting success.

Carnegie Steel Company (US Steel) was founded by Andrew Carnegie, an immigrant whose first job was working as a bobbin boy in a cotton factory for 20 cents a day. He built Carnegie Steel Company into one of the largest corporations in America, and when he retired in 1901, he had a fortune of a half billion dollars. He felt it was a sin to die rich, and wrote in his *Gospel of Wealth* that rich men are trustees of their wealth with a fiduciary responsibility to use it for public good. Consequently, he committed more than $350,000,000 in his lifetime—building schools, universities, and libraries all across America.

In addition to sharing his wealth with the public, he shared it with those on his payroll. With the exception of the Homestead Strike,[5] which occurred while he was out of the country, his labor relations were always good. He often said, "Capital, labor and employer [are] a three-legged stool, none before or after the others, all equally indispensable." He once wrote, "I believe that higher wages to men who respect their employers and are happy and contented are a good investment, yielding, indeed, big dividends."[6] Over 29 of his executives became millionaires in their own rights.

Carnegie was shrewd and sharp, but fair, honest, and compassionate. He enjoyed making money and sharing its benefits with others. At a time when industrialists were universally characterized as "robber barons," honor was dearer to him than making a quick dollar. He demonstrated it through action, and reaped the rewards of success.

The Freeman Companies grew from a party decorating company in 1923 to become one of the largest staging and decorating corporations in the United States. In 1981, President Don Freeman announced an Employee Stock Ownership Plan for the company to transfer ownership from the family to employees. Today, most ESOP's are done by public companies to avert a hostile takeover. However, Freeman was a family-owned company, and the sole reason was to reward the employees who had made the company grow and prosper.

How well is the program working? Sales in 1981 were $45,000,000, and by 1989 they had soared to $190,000,000—up 422 percent! By the end of the 1989 fiscal year, 23 percent of the corporate stock had been placed in employee hands. The ESOP had worked so well the family voted to transfer an additional 23 percent in the decade of the 1990s! Freeman didn't just talk about making a commitment—he honored it.

Are You a Person of Honor?

Would you like a quick and easy way of determining your own sense of honor, or that of your co-workers or employees? Simply answer this question: Who are your five biggest heroes or heroines? You can tell a lot about yourself or others by the answers you get!

Before you read farther, stop now and list your five favorite heroes and heroines. They can be from the pages of history, of faith, or of fiction—don't stop and think about it, just list them right off the top of your head!

My Five All Time Heroes

1.
2.
3.
4.
5.

Look at your list of heroes. What does your list reveal about yourself and your sense of honor and integrity? Do you try to emulate those you admire? Most people do!

The problem with honor, as we said at the onset, is that some people have no clear idea of the definition. When Harvard Business School began teaching ethics as well as business principles, John McArthur, dean of the school, started encouraging students not to "go through life focused only on number one." According to a *Wall Street Journal* article, Albert Gordon, a Harvard fund-raiser and chairman emeritus of Kidder Peabody, said, "I hope they don't take the ethics issue too far...they run the risk that some students could decide to go to other schools in the future."

Dean McArthur added an ethics question to the admission test. It asks students to explain how they have managed an ethical dilemma they have experienced. Laura Gordon Fisher, the school's admissions director says, "It's amazing how many people admit they've never experienced a moral dilemma. Some applicants want to know if they should fabricate one."

Either those students live in a "kinder, gentler world" than the rest of us or they lack a moral compass to tell them when they face a dilemma.

The Bottom Line

People today want action anchored by integrity in their leaders, associates, and friends. Everyone wishes everyone else was that way, but it must begin with each of us. If our nation and our organizations are to continue to thrive, or even survive, in a fast-paced future that is marked by increased demands and rapid change, we must create a foundation of honor, integrity, and commitment. Doing so provides that trust, respect, and sense of constancy that serves as a compass to guide us in tough times. Competence, what we can do, is an important contributor to success. But character, what we are, determines our direction. These ideas may sound simplistic, but profound truths often appear simplistic to skeptics.

People have a right to be skeptical about integrity. They've been lied to and misled before. How do you convince others that you're serious about your commitment? Try saying, "On my honor, I will"—then do it! That, of course, is the key: **doing it.** An adage says, "The road to hell is paved with good intentions." *Thinking* a good game is not the same as *playing* a good game. Thinking a good deed is not the same as doing a good deed. Inaction cannot be compensated for by thinking, "Wasn't it nice of me to have *thought* about doing that!" We may judge ourselves by our intentions, but others evaluate us by our actions.

Once you put hands and feet on your commitment and follow through, you'll become known as a person of honor—because you'll be a person of honor! You won't have to talk about your honor, other people will talk about it instead. As D.L. Moody said, "We are told to let our light shine, and if it does, we won't need to tell anybody it does. Lighthouses don't fire cannons to call attention to their shining—they just shine."

SIX STEPS TO BECOMING
A PERSON OF HONOR

1. Establish the habit of focusing on what's right rather than who's right.
2. Develop a list of honorable heroes and heroines. Learn everything you can about them. Make these people your personal "board of directors" and when you're faced with a moral dilemma, ask yourself what they would do.
3. Consciously associate with people of integrity. Seek out co-workers, neighbors, mentors, and employers who demonstrate their integrity and commitment. They'll be easy to spot once you know what to look for. They'll have a reputation for integrity, responsibility, and helping others.
4. Regularly spend time in self-evaluation. Evaluate your actions against the actions of other honorable and committed individuals when you're faced with a tough decision.
5. Accept complete responsibility for your actions, especially when it's convenient to blame others. Actively accepting responsibility forces us to evaluate the impact of our decisions prior to our actions.
6. Stand by your beliefs, even when they appear unpopular. Compromise on implementation and interpretation, never on principles. Whenever possible, work for solutions that meet everyone's needs, but never sacrifice the integrity and honesty of your beliefs on the altar of convenience.

"ON MY HONOR, I WILL"

You will find a fill-in-the-blank section at the end of each remaining chapter. Its purpose is to allow you the opportunity to make your own commitments. We hope you'll use the time and space to reflect on things you're currently doing that are consistent with the material covered in each chapter. Most importantly, we hope you'll set specific goals for yourself in areas where you want to grow or improve.

In the space provided, list commitments you wish to make regarding your personal honor and actions.

NOTES

CHAPTER 3

DO MY BEST

"Lives of great men all remind us
We too can make our lives sublime
And departing, leave behind us
Footprints on the sands of time."
-Henry Wadsworth Longfellow
"A Psalm of Life"

While we appreciate Longfellow's sentiments, few people will leave footprints on the sands of time that more than a handful will ever notice. Columbus, explorer of the New World, left footprints in the New World and opened the way for exploration and colonization. Schweitzer, missionary doctor to Africa, left footprints in unexplored jungles. Chuck Yeagar, the first man to fly faster than the speed of sound, left footprints in the sky. Neil Armstrong, first man on the moon, left footprints on the lunar sands of the Sea of Tranquillity. Albert Einstein, developer of the theory of relativity, left footprints leading into the wide universe.

We could go on and on, naming names like Louis Pasteur, Jonas Salk, Florence Nightingale, Booker T. Washington, George Washington Carver, and Martin Luther King, Jr. Who wouldn't like to be a genuine American hero, even if it were only for the fifteen minutes Andy Warhol promised? We may have neither the ability nor the opportunity to be a hero to millions, but each of us has the opportunity to do our best every day. And, by doing so, we leave our own, albeit humble, footsteps on the sands of time.

We may never be counted among the world's best, but we should always be counted on to *do our best*. Each of us is being watched by others to see how we handle temptations and challenges. When those around us see us doing our best day in and day out, we inspire them to do the same. If we inspire others by example, then in our own way, we are leaving footprints on the sands of time.

We often associate greatness with fame. We glamorize others' actions and assign them hero status. There's nothing wrong with heroes. We need more of them as role models in our world. But, we must not think less of ourselves because we have not or cannot achieve hero status. The fame we associate with heroism requires more than greatness—it often requires special circumstances. Could Audie Murphy have become the most-decorated American soldier if he had been drafted in peacetime? What if Mary Lou Retton had been born before the modern Olympics? What if George Washington Carver had been born in an area that did not grow sweet potatoes and peanuts? Could Roger Staubach have been a hero if he'd been born in a place or time where football wasn't the king of sports? Of course not. So while part of being a hero—of being the best—comes from within, some of it comes from without. For this reason, you can't judge yourself harshly just because situations do not come along to prove your heroic qualities.

Most of the people we call heroes were going about their business, doing their best when the special circumstances arrived. An old motivational speaker liked to say, "When opportunity knocks, you have to jump up and answer the door!" "How do you know it's opportunity?" someone in the audience would invariably ask. He would answer, "You don't. You have to keep jumping!"

Roger Staubach, writing in *Winning Strategies in Selling*, talked about the role events outside our control play in success. A quarterback has no control over the field position his team has when he gets the ball. He said if the defensive team gives you the ball in good field position, then you're in a good position to be a hero. On the other hand, if you get the ball deep in your own territory, being a hero isn't as easy.

In life, some of us inherit better field position than others. If your ancestors ran from 5' 6" to 5' 8" tall, you're in poor field position to become a professional basketball star. There have been short basketball stars, Spud Webb is an excellent example. Although less than 5' 8" tall, he is a true superstar and has won the NBA dunking contest against players a foot and a half taller! Basketball today is a game of giants. A player of less than average height, like Spud, has his work cut out to be a hero. Spud couldn't do a thing about his "field position," all he could do was do his best—and that was enough to make him a superstar.

That's the point. Good field position is a blessing, but poor field position can be overcome. For example, if you have musical interests and are born into a musical family, you are in excellent field position for musical achievement. If you have musical interests and are born into a family who can't afford lessons, you have poorer field position, but you can still excel—as evidenced by the success of singer Ray Charles.

We each have the ability to be the best we can be, and in doing our best, we become great even if we don't become famous. Should a surgeon give up his practice just because he or she isn't the world's leading surgeon? Should an actor forsake the theater because he isn't as famous as Lawrence Olivier? Must a pilot turn in his wings because he'll never be a "top gun"? Should a mother place her children in an orphanage because she'll never be "Mother-of-the-Year"? Should a salesperson resign because he or she will never be the top salesperson in the company? Should a teacher abandon her class because she has no geniuses to inspire? Of course not! We work within the field position we have. We overcome obstacles, or we go around them. We give each situation, each challenge, and each opportunity our best shot.

We become great by using our motives, means, and opportunities to continually work toward being our best. If the special circumstances present themselves, we may achieve fame, but that's icing on the cake. The true superstar was great before he or she became famous, and many famous people are not great at anything.

A golfing buddy once lost a round by 12 strokes and was ecstatic! Even though he had lost, he had played the best round of golf of his life. He was happy because he wasn't trying to beat his opponent's score—he was trying to beat his own best score.

Being the best was not as important to him as doing his best. The same is true with each of us. You may never be the best—but you can be the best you can be. You can be better tomorrow than you are today and better next week than you are tomorrow. It takes time, training, and dedication—but every individual can do it! You can succeed because you're not in a game where there's only one winner and everyone else is a loser. You're in the game of life, a game in which everyone can be a winner. You're not competing against the best in the world, you're competing against your own previous best effort. Leaders know the only record they're trying to beat is their own.

Film star Ingrid Bergman, in her autobiography, *My Story*, relates that she was always driven to do her best in every scene. Many times, she insisted in redoing a scene that everyone else thought was fine the way it was. Finally, she'd say, "Well, that was good-but I'll do better later." She said it so often on one film that the crew began good-naturedly calling her "Betterlater!"

A friend of the authors has children who are competitive swimmers. Before a meet, he tells them, "It isn't important whether or not you win a ribbon. It's not important that you be the best—what's important is that you do your best. If you do that, your mother and I will be proud of you, and more importantly, you'll be proud of yourselves."

In our careers and our relationships with others, we can be proud of ourselves when we do our best. We may fail to reach the goals we set for ourselves, but we'll "fail forward." That is, we will fail reaching toward the mark. We will come closer to the mark than we ever did before.

And when we fail forward, chances are that we will ultimately go the full distance.

Doing Your Best Every Day —The Organizational Imperative

Until the Korean war, Americans viewed themselves as the biggest and best at everything. We had entered the nineteenth century certain we had a "manifest destiny" to stretch our borders from sea to shining sea. We flexed our muscles in the Spanish-American War, then entered World War I confident we could "lick the Hun." We emerged from that war as a world leader. In World War II, we entered confident we could fight enemies on two sides of the globe and win. We emerged from that war as the dominant world power. While the rest of the world lay in shambles, America was strong, rich, free, and confident.

Our optimism carried over into our business and commerce. The industrial revolution achieved its greatest moments in this country. The inventors and inventions that sparked the information age were "Made in the U.S.A." and those words defined quality. During the 1950s, "Made in Japan" meant junk to us. Then the Japanese decided they needed some American know-how to re-build and compete. They hired American, W. Edwards Deming, to teach them the true meaning of quality and continuous improvement.

What happened next? Japanese businesses began concentrating on quality. Meanwhile, many American businesses began thinking that quick returns were more important than quality. Consequently, many American businesses began "doing what's required" instead of "doing what's best." Performance slipped, bringing down quality, dependability, and service. Workers in other parts of the world began producing to the American standard of quality at a lower cost. Our balance of payments shifted out of kilter as our fellow citizens began buying foreign goods that were of equal or greater quality and lower in cost.

We saw the result of our actions, but too often we failed to focus on "what's wrong," preferring instead to find "who's wrong." Management blamed workers, lamenting, "Workers have changed! They don't care about a day's work for a day's pay anymore." Workers blamed management, claiming, "Management is getting what they deserve. We want to do a good job, but they're more interested in quantity than quality."

While we argued and pointed fingers, "Made in Japan" became synonymous with high quality and value in the minds of many. Meanwhile, some have come to consider "Made in the U.S.A." synonymous with low quality and poor value.

Today, we are sensing a resurgence of America's traditional commitment to quality, service, and value. It has again become fashionable to "do my best." Words like integrity, quality, excellence, and service are again becoming the maxims by which we manage and lead. Organizations that are making their mark in the global marketplace have relearned and determined to live by the principle of continuous improvement and doing their best everyday.

History provides us many examples of American leaders who focused on doing their best to fill a need or meet a challenge.

Edison, who failed thousands of times before perfecting the incandescent light bulb, taught us the value of innovation, research, and persistence. After years of futile attempts, Chester Carlson invented the first xerographic copier—teaching us the value of persistence and belief in a goal.

Had either of these men focused only on "being the best" they might never have achieved their goal. They might have given up and tried to take an easier road to the top. Instead, they did their best each day and eventually succeeded.

A desire to **be** the best encourages expedience to reach a specific position at a given point in time. A commitment to **doing** one's best every day leads to long-term excellence. As the philosopher Socrates said, "Wealth does not bring about excellence, but excellence brings about wealth and all other public and private blessings for a man."

Not every individual who focuses on doing their best revolutionizes business, but every individual who focuses on doing their best can and does make a contribution. Our "footprints on the sands of time" may not appear in history books, but they can influence the opportunities of others. Who's to say that a business leader doing his or her best won't provide the environment for a major technological breakthrough? Who's to say that a parent doing his or her best isn't shaping the life of a future U.S. President? At the very least, they are helping to shape their child's values and ideas, and that can be an important gift to the world. Do you think Gerald Ford's Scoutmaster knew that he was influencing the life of a future U.S. President?

We have an opportunity, as individuals and organizations, to leave our footprints on the sands of time by doing our best each day. Einstein had a teacher. Lincoln had a role model. Carver had someone who instilled in him a desire to learn. Retton had a coach. Without these often unknown people doing their best, we might never have been influenced by those who became the best!

Why don't we each do our best? The sad truth is, many want to leave the difficult tasks to someone else, focusing on expedience at the expense of achievement. A few others find it easier to let others do it all and reap the rewards. There have always been some shirkers, but it wasn't until the time of the Korean War that shirking became prevalent in America.

During the Korean Conflict, the Army found that 100 percent of the fighting was done by 30 percent of the combat soldiers. This doesn't include the support and supply personnel—a staggering 70 percent of those soldiers who were in combat situations never fired their weapons. A study showed there were four primary reasons why most soldiers chose not to fight:

1. **They lacked confidence in their weapons.** The U.S. Army had the most sophisticated, reliable, advanced weapons in the world, but their soldiers lacked confidence in them! They were afraid they would get into a difficult situation and their weapons would fail to protect them.
2. **They liked to rely on heavy artillery and aerial bombardment.** In this war, America had air superiority. The troops in the field thought it was better to just wait and let the planes and the big guns do the fighting. It took less time, trouble and risk to call for bombardment than it did to fight. Besides, the guns were heavy, cumbersome and had heavy recoil. (We

tried to negate this objection in Vietnam by going from a .30 to a .22 caliber in our main battle rifle and from .45 to 9mm [.38 caliber] in sidearms.)

3. **They didn't like to expose themselves to enemy fire.** They felt the enemy would fire back at anyone who fired at them. If you stayed down and kept low, you might go unnoticed.

4. **They liked to take the line of least resistance.** Doing nothing is always easier than doing something. It was easier to hole up and wait than it was to move forward and perhaps fail.

This survey in no way depreciates actions of the many heroic soldiers who displayed gallantry and bravery in the face of the enemy in Korea. It merely points out that many are content if their outfit "is the best." They do not feel a personal obligation to "do their best" in order to keep it that way.

Our purpose is not to evaluate our national performance on the battlefield, but our performance on the competitive field of life and work. Yet there is something to be learned from our study of the fighting men in Korea. Today, many individuals and organizations are not "doing their best" because of similar reasons.

1. **They lack confidence in their weapons.** They aren't certain their products and their processes are as good as their competitors'. They aren't certain of their corporate or personal commitment to "be the best."

2. **They like to rely on heavy artillery and aerial bombardment to accomplish their objectives.** How do we "bomb" our competition in business? With

marketing muscle, advertising, and promotion. Many sales people feel the solution doesn't lie in their own hard work but in better ads. Many production people feel the solution lies not in their producing a better product but in someone hiring better sales people.

3. **They don't like to expose themselves to enemy fire.** If you move out aggressively, your enemies will notice you. Some hang back hoping to "hide in a crack where the competition can't find them." While it does make sense to pick your opportunities, once you're in the contest, you must face your competition head-on in order to survive. Unfortunately, even successful companies often reward not failing more than they reward initiative. Therefore, their "troops" hesitate to stick their necks out, feeling, "If I don't risk anything, I won't lose anything."

4. **They like to take the line of least resistance.** It takes less effort to fail than it does to succeed. No one questions you if you do it the way you have always done it. If you try something new and it doesn't work, you have to explain and then you might lapse into reason number 3.

Competition Makes Us Better

How do we instill the desire to "do our best" in ourselves and others? One way is through competition. Healthy competition challenges us to new heights, and helps build the desire to do our best. What do you do if you're head-and-shoulders above the competition? Well, then you compete against your own best efforts.

A sixteenth century samurai named Miyamoto Musashi had the problem of being so much better than his competition that he found himself bored. He had became a swordsman of legendary proportions, and once defeated 150 samurai in a single battle. Like gunfighters in the American West, the number of people willing to challenge him grew along with his reputation. Scarcely a week went by that some up-and-coming "sword-slinger" didn't challenge him to a duel. Musashi grew tired of killing, yet he could not refuse a challenge without losing face. Finally, he compromised by carving himself a wooden sword and fighting with that!

By using a wooden sword, he was able to rise to the challenge, keep his competitive spirit, save face, and also save the lives of his adversaries. He never stopped proving he was the best swordsman in Japan—and lived to die of natural causes.

Healthy competition is a great tool for pushing ourselves and others toward doing their best, but certain kinds of competition can be unhealthy. "Winning is everything" has, unfortunately, often been interpreted as winning at all costs. The kind of competition that focuses on competing against others is neither healthy nor friendly. It builds adversaries rather than respected competitors, and it is a major force behind the lack of trust and cynicism that exists in many businesses. If we do "whatever it takes" to win in one area, what's to keep us from doing the same in another?

Healthy competition comes when we compete with others rather than against them. Leaders approach life and work with a desire to "do my best every day." That focuses the competition internally instead of just externally. It encourages us to compete with ourselves, not against others. It enables us to be team players—because if we're competing against ourselves, then each person on the team can emerge a winner—even if the team should lose.

What does it take to do your best today and every day? It takes five things: **purpose, responsibility, commitment, flexibility,** and **support.** Let's examine each separately.

1. Purpose (You must have a reason to do your best.) When Alice met the Cheshire Cat in *Alice in Wonderland*, she asked, "Would you tell me, please, which way I ought to go from here?"

"That depends a good deal on where you want to get to," said the Cat.

"I don't much care where…," said Alice.

"Then it doesn't matter which way you go," said the Cat.

The Chesire Cat's point was well taken. If we don't know where we're going, then one path is as good as another. It is only when we have a purpose and a destination that the road we take become important.

The Roman philosopher Seneca wrote in *On the Happy Life*: "First, therefore, we must seek what it is we are aiming at; then we must look about for the road by which we can reach it most quickly, and on the journey itself, if only we are on the right path, we shall discover how much of the distance we overcome each day, and how much nearer we are to the goal toward which we are urged by natural desire."

Dennis McCuistion, consultant, author[1] and talk show host, often asks people to define and write down their mission in addition to their goals. An individual's mission, like that of an organization, provides the overriding purpose against which goals can be evaluated. Doing your best, for the sake of doing your best, is difficult to maintain over long periods. Purpose provides direction and internal motivation.

2. Commitment (You must tenaciously work toward your goal.) Commitment is what occurs when desire and self-discipline come together. It's an inward desire to achieve your best because you want to, not because you have to. It is commitment that keeps you going in spite of discouragement, disillusionment, and defeat. It is commitment that keeps you practicing, preparing, and producing when it would be easier to call it quits.

Calvin Coolidge, thirtieth President of the United States, had this to say about the importance of commitment:

"Press on: Nothing in the world can take the place of persistence. Talent will not; nothing is more common than unsuccessful individuals with talent. Genius will not; unrewarded genius is almost a proverb. Education will not; the world is full of educated derelicts. Persistence and determination alone are omnipotent."

Occasional brilliance does not consistently win races. Consistent effort is the mark of true commitment. An admirer once told Van Cliburn, "I'd give my life to be able to play the piano like that!" Cliburn replied, "I did."

Desire comes from within, but the self-discipline required to demonstrate your commitment must be learned. Consider establishing a daily plan to help you develop successful habits. The plan should include specific goals, both immediate and long-range, that move you forward. It should also include the activities you need to perform every day to meet your goals. The first few days will be difficult. Remember how you felt on the second day of your new exercise program? But, after a month or so, you'll find yourself with new habits that propel you toward your desired purpose. Many people desire to be their best. It is the only those who combine desire with self-discipline who have the commitment to really be their best.

3. Responsibility (You must hold yourself accountable for your choices.) Successful individuals understand cause and effect relationships: we reap what we sow. In computer jargon, the catch-phrase is GI/GO. Usually, GI/GO means "garbage in/garbage out," but it can also mean "good in/good out." The interesting thing about sowing and reaping is that the harvest is inevitably larger than the planting. If we plant beans in our garden, we get beans back—multiplied. If we were foolish enough to plant thistles in our garden, we would reap thistles—multiplied.

When we take personal responsibility for our successes and failures, we begin looking for "ways" instead of "outs." We lose the ability to learn from our mistakes when we rationalize failures. Begin replacing excuses like, "They told me to" and "It's not my fault because..." with winning phrases like, "I made a mistake, but I have learned..." and "It was my responsibility."

4. Flexibility (You must be willing to creatively adapt to change.) There are seven words that shackle organizations and people to the past. They are: *"We've never done it this way before!"* Benjamin Franklin said, "Don't look for the birds of this year in the nests of the last." Today, change doesn't just come annually, but monthly, weekly, and even daily. Tradition has its place in our core values, but hidebound tradition can cause us to lose our competitive edge as organizations and individuals. One client described his organization as 33 years of tradition unmarred by progress! We have to be flexible enough to break with tradition if we're going to turn obstacles into opportunities.

Beethoven began to lose his hearing in his twenties, yet he had learned the sound of music so well that he could compose in his mind. Some of his greatest masterpieces were created after the composer was unable to hear a single note of music! Milton, the poet, went blind—yet he taught himself to compose in his head and dictated to his daughters. Wilma Rudolph wore leg braces as a child, yet she overcame her handicap to become a great athlete. As Renoir's arthritis became so bad he couldn't hold a paint brush, he had friends tie a brush to his hand—and continued painting. Moreover, he continued painting masterpieces!

When you face adversity, be flexible and open to alternate routes. As Zig Ziglar says, "When life hands you a lemon, make lemonade."

5. Support (You must have others on your team.) A good quarterback can help make a football team great, but a team is more than a quarterback. No matter how good a player is, he can't play all the positions. When time is running out, it's good to know that there are others to call on for support who share your commitment and your mission. The quarterback may get most of the attention, but he is quick to remind everyone of his support team; because without it, he'd never be able to move the ball.

The value of support is shown by successful programs such as Weight Watchers and Alcoholics Anonymous

(AA). In AA, each member is assigned a support person because they realize that the fight to do their best every day is often overwhelming.

In your own fight to do your best every day, family, friends, co-workers, subordinates, and bosses are good sources of support. In the unlikely event no one is available to support you, make finding a support team a priority. Enlist the help of a mentor at work. Join a group where people have similar interests and problems. Remember, the best athletes have coaches to help them maintain focus and improve. Don't try to "go it alone" or fail to hold up your end of the bargain by helping others as you've been helped.

LEADERSHIP IN ACTION: SAM WALTON

Forbes magazine named Sam Walton the "richest man in America" in October of 1985, but the journey to being the best began many years earlier—with a desire to do his best.

Sam Walton's father and mother were his earliest influences. He described his father as "an awfully hard worker who got up early, put in long hours, and was honest."[2] His mother, Nan, responded to the hard times of the Depression by starting a small milk business. She motivated Sam by telling him to be the best he could at anything he undertook.

These early influences taught Sam Walton the value of honesty, hard work, and doing his best. He became an Eagle Scout at age 13, the youngest in the State of Missouri at that time. Walton was active in a variety of sports, and extracurricular and student leadership activities throughout high school and college. Young Sam impressed people even then. But, Sam Walton the master merchant was still a few years away. His success would be influenced by yet others committed to doing their best.

Walton's first job after graduation from college was with JCPenney as a management trainee. While Sam was a great salesman, he was not particularly good at the paperwork aspects of the job. Fortunately, he worked for Duncan Majors in Des Moines, Iowa. Walton described Majors as "a great motivator who was proudest of having trained more managers than anybody else in the country."[3] Majors was credited with getting Walton excited about retail. That excitement first showed itself at a Ben Franklin variety store in Newport, Arkansas.

After a two year stint in the Army, Sam Walton purchased his first store for $25,000, $20,000 of which was borrowed from his father-in-law. His goal was to make it the most profitable variety store in the state within five years. After purchasing the business he discovered two immediate obstacles: he had bought into a poorly negotiated building lease and his competitor across the street already had sales that were twice the levels of his store. Yet, through purpose, commitment, flexibility, and support from others, Walton did his best and achieved his goals. He continually focused on improvements and innovations to serve his customers. Five years later, the Ben Franklin store in Newport, Arkansas, was number one for sales and profit in the six state region.

The story of Sam Walton is a profile in commitment to doing one's best. Charlie Baum, an early Wal-Mart partner said, "I've known Sam since his first store in Newport, Arkansas, and I believe that money is, in some respects, almost immaterial to him. What motivates the man is the desire to absolutely be on top of the heap."[4] Sam Walton believed in healthy competition, but most important he believed in using it as motivation to be his best. His life and achievements stand as a memorial to both what is possible when we commit to doing our best and to the impact we can have on the lives of others.

"Doing my best" is often viewed as a product, but in reality it is a process. Winning athletes, artists, performers, managers, and business leaders continually focus on the process of doing their best. Consistently putting these five steps in practice sets them on an exciting path of growth, development, and success.

Continually look for new ways to accomplish your goals. Don't settle for the way you've always done it. The pace of change in today's world will make yesterday's solutions obsolete. Continuous improvement is a must for people and organizations who want to do their best. Consider new opportunities for learning and development as a way to keep your ideas fresh.

Since 1909, Boy Scouts have been pledging, "On my honor, I will do my best...." Scouts give their word to keep on doing their best—to be all that they can be. We become our best when we preach doing our best. As Aristotle said, "We are what we repeatedly do. Excellence then, is not an act, but a habit."

Get in the habit of doing your best. Begin saying out loud, "I will do my best." My best what? My best work. My best to be a good spouse to my mate, parent to my kids, kid to my parents, neighbor to my neighbor, citizen to my country, employee to my organization and leader to my employees.

Doing one's best is a way of demonstrating commitment. Commitment is the single most important factor in becoming a long term success both professionally and personally.

"ON MY HONOR, I WILL"

In the space provided, list some commitments you wish to make in order to do your best.

NOTES

CHAPTER 4
TO DO MY DUTY

"I slept and dreamed that life was beauty.
I woke—and found that life was duty."
- Ellen Surgis Hooper
"Beauty and Duty"

For many people, duty comes as a rude awakening...usually sometime between puberty and adulthood. As children, duties are often imposed on us by others. We feel that life would beautiful adventure of fun and excitement if we could only get out from under the collective thumbs of our parents and teachers. When the day finally comes and we're on our own, we find we have duties of our own—duties to our friends, to ourselves, to our families, to our peers.

Some duties are legal, such as our duty to pay taxes, serve on juries, or serve our country in times of national emergency. Other duties are moral, such as to be a person of integrity, to provide and care for our families, to be all we can be, to pull our own weight. There are times when each of us wishes we could "live for beauty," but successful individuals know that the ultimate freedom comes when they do their duty to themselves and others at home, in the community, and on the job.

So why do we have a shortage of responsibility takers? How can we cultivate a sense of duty in a world where society's feelings and actions were summed up one day when we heard an executive complain, "I think our number one problem is that nobody wants to take responsibility for anything—but don't quote me!"

The easy answer is that values are shifting, people are changing, and everyone is busy chasing the all mighty dollar. These things may be true, but they are often merely excuses for failure. We need solutions for success.

America and American business has suffered from a shortage of people willing to take responsibility. Managers and employees alike sometimes find it easier to hide behind the rules rather than accept responsibility. Some seem more interested in "not losing" a battle than in winning it. Bill Hampton, President of Management Alternatives, a pioneer in developing computerized route distribution systems for the food and beverage industry, observes, "There are companies that would spend ten thousand dollars to try to save a dime and wouldn't spend a dime to try and make ten thousand dollars!" These organizations and individuals have made the choice to do only the minimum required, to define duty and responsibility in the most narrow terms. Successful leaders and individuals, people who have made and will continue to make their mark on our lives, see duty differently. They see duty as the responsibility to work for everyone's benefit. In the organization, that means working for the benefit of:

- **Shareholders**
- **Customers**
- **Employees**
- **Suppliers**
- **Community**

In private life, that means working for the benefit of:

- **Family**
- **Friends**
- **Self**

As leaders, it is important that we do our duty, and that we teach and inspire others to do theirs as well. John D. Rockefeller, Jr., speaking for the United Service Organization in 1941 said, "I believe that every right implies a responsibility; every opportunity, an obligation; every possession, a duty."

Robert E. Lee said, "Duty is the sublimest word in our language. Do your duty in all things. You cannot do more. You should never wish to do less."

The Importance Of Making Choices

Leaders do not choose whether or not to do their duty. They only get to choose how the act is accomplished. If we have honor, we approach our duty with a high level of commitment. We are not content to just "do our job," we want to do more than our job. We want to do what's right—even if something is lost in the process.

LEADERSHIP IN ACTION: JOHNSON & JOHNSON

A good example is the action taken by Johnson and Johnson during the Tylenol crisis in 1982. Seven people died when an individual—not an employee—tampered with Tylenol capsules in the Chicago areas. Blame was not attributed to Johnson and Johnson, but the company voluntarily pulled the product off the shelves and kept it off until they had developed tamper-resistant packaging. Fortunately for Johnson & Johnson, they not only did the right thing, they were perceived as having done the right thing. The company suffered a short-term loss in profits, but their immediate sense of duty to their customers and the public resulted in a long-term increase in Tylenol's market share.

Johnson and Johnson didn't have to wonder how to react when the crisis came, they had a 40 year old corporate credo, a philosophy that established the company's priorities and defined its duties and responsibilities:

> **We believe our first responsibility** is to the doctors, nurses, and patients, to mothers and all others who use our products and services. In meeting their needs, everything we do must be of high quality. We must constantly strive to reduce our costs in order to maintain reasonable prices. Customers'

orders must be serviced promptly and accurately. Our suppliers and distributors must have an opportunity to make a fair profit.

We are responsible to our employees, the men and women who work with us throughout the world. Everyone must be considered as an individual. We must respect their dignity and recognize their merit. They must have a sense of security in their jobs. Compensation must be fair and adequate, and working conditions, clean, orderly, and safe. Employees must feel free to make suggestions and complaints. There must be equal opportunity for employment, development, and advancement for those qualified. We must provide competent management, and their actions must be just and ethical.

We are responsible to the communities in which we live and work and to the world community as well. We must be good citizens—support good works and charities and bear our fair share of taxes. We must encourage civic improvements and better health and education. We must maintain in good order the property we are privileged to use, protecting the environment and natural resources.

Our final responsibility is to our stockholders. Business must make a sound profit. We must experiment with new ideas. Research must be carried on, innovative programs developed, and mistakes paid for. New equipment must be purchased, new facilities provided and new products launched. When we operate according to these principles, the stockholders should realize a fair return.

Did Johnson and Johnson "do their duty?" They went above and beyond. They were up front with the media, with the government, with the consumers—and both the people and the press appreciated it. On February 21, 1986, the *Miami News* contrasted Johnson & Johnson's actions with manufacturer A.H. Robins in these words:

"By way of odious comparison: In 1974, after three years and 2.86 million sales. A.H. Robins stopped selling its Dalkon Shield intrauterine device. By then, the evidence was mounting that the shield was life-threatening to users."

"Robins didn't recall the shield. Instead, it spent the next ten years in court shuffling and ducking responsibility. Federal judge Miles Lord of Minneapolis called the performance, 'corporate irresponsibility at its meanest.' "

The *Miami News* article continued, "It [Johnson & Johnson] lost $250 million in sales after the previous cyanide scare, in 1982. But the company rebuilt its market, at least partly because it treats people as human beings and not as contributors to its bottom line." The article talked about J&J's move to New Brunswick, New Jersey, and the fact that they had poured millions of dollars of its own money into helping the city attract Urban Development Action Grant funds to modernize and beautify the city's downtown area, paid for training sessions in beautification and revitalization, etc. They used this information to create another contrast in corporate culture. Again, quoting the *Miami News*, "While this was going on, only five miles away in...Manville, N.J., the Manville Corp., the asbestos maker, faced an outburst of damage even bigger than the Dalkon Shield's. So Manville...filed for reorganization under Chapter 11 of the bankruptcy laws...federal judge Jerome H. Sarokin of Newark says Manville 'manipulated the judicial system so as to delay to thousands of claimants and deny completely to some their day in court to present asbestos-related injuries.' "

The article concludes, "J&J is in business to make money. It has done that very well. But when the going gets tough, the corporation gets human, and that makes it something special in the...business world."

The lesson from J&J is clear: If you do what is right, people will eventually notice it. If others don't do right, you'll look better for the comparison.

LEADERSHIP IN ACTION: NATIONAL GYPSUM COMPANY

In the mid 1970s, National Gypsum Company, the second-largest supplier of wallboard in North America, forecast that the coming building boom would be centered in the South. Therefore, they began investigating the possibility of moving the headquarters for their Gold Bond wallboard division from Buffalo, New York, to a more centrally-located city in their primary growth market.

When the announcement of a site selection was made, the press in Buffalo responded negatively, stating that the announcement was a new low in corporate relations, despite the company's obvious attempt to make the best of a difficult decision. The company made every effort to balance the needs of all parties concerned. National did their duty to shareholders by making a good business decision. They did their duty to customers by positioning the company to offer quality products at a reasonable price (which can only be done by being close to markets). They did their duty to suppliers by remaining in business so commerce could continue. They did their duty to employees by moving the vast majority to Charlotte, North Carolina, assigning some to other operations, and allowing still others to take early retirement. A small minority of employees held positions not continued, and they were paid liberal retirement benefits.

There are times, of course, when duty takes you through a veritable mine field of conflicting wants and needs. A good case in point was the LBO (Leveraged Buy Out) of National Gypsum Company in 1986. At that time, National Gypsum produced not only wallboard, but floor covering, glass, and other related home building and remodeling products. These are all commodities, driven by the law of supply and demand, and the company was experiencing good sales, good profits, and had a long history of paying good dividends to shareholders. However, price/earning multiples were low by NYSE standards, which brought the company to the attention of corporate raiders.

In early November 1985, rumors were mounting of a hostile takeover of National Gypsum Company by the Belzberg family of Canada. The company had earlier resisted takeover attempts by both Victor Posner and Louisiana-Pacific. Since hostile takeovers are historically made by leveraging the future of the company to cover the debt incurred, John P. Hayes, CEO of National Gypsum, had to face the problem of ensuring that shareholders received the greatest value possible for their investment while also preserving the company's long-term viability.

Hayes said, "There were more than economic considerations involved in our decision. Many people had spent virtually all their working lives with National Gypsum Company. Our associates and customers had become our friends as well. An unfriendly takeover would have had a tremendous negative impact on the company and our customers, and the futures of our employees would have been severely threatened."

On November 25, 1985, a management-led investor group, known as Aancor Holdings, Inc, initiated an offer to National Gypsum shareholders for $40.50 cash and $17 face value of 15½ percent redeemable discount debentures. The value of this offer was significantly greater than the highest market value ever attained by the company's common stock.[1]

To protect shareholders' interests, the Board of Directors created a fairness committee that hired Salomon Brothers and Dillon Reed to render fairness opinions regarding the offer. On January 7, 1986, the investor group proposed a revised merger proposal of $41 in cash and $17 in debentures, which received the approval of National's Board of Directors with the final decision to be made by shareholders at the April 10 meeting.

For three months, both the financial community and the media felt the management-led leveraged buy out was a "done deal." Then at 3:25 p.m. on April 8, 1986, the phone on Jack Hayes desk rang. Sanford Sigoloff, Chairman of Wickes, came on the line and said they were putting out a press release at that time indicating they were going to make a tender offer for all the stock of National Gypsum at $54 a share.

The reasoning was that an upturn in the building business made the company potentially more valuable. Still, as Jack Hayes recalls, "I couldn't have been more surprised. First of all, Wickes was a large customer of ours. I felt an acquisition by Wickes would alienate many of National Gypsum's customers. On top of that, Wickes had just come out of bankruptcy and was a most unlikely suitor. I shared this with Sandy, and he indicated it was strictly a financial deal and shouldn't affect the marketing operations of the business. Again, I was surprised and somewhat startled to hear he didn't think a financial deal of this magnitude would affect marketing."

The easy road for National's management would have been acquiesce to Wickes' demands. The shareholders would have received more for the stock than it had ever sold for. National Gypsum's top management was nearing retirement age, had a large block of stock, and there must have been some thought about "taking the money and running." Management, however, agonized over their duty not only to shareholders, but to customers, employees, suppliers, and the communities they served.

In the end, management fought the hostile takeover and won. True, in so doing, they drove up the debt of the company, effectively mortgaging the future. True, it meant divesting some divisions. "Well," you may well ask, "then what was the purpose of fighting the takeover?"

The leader's duty is to balance the long-term needs of all constituencies. To mortgage the long-term needs of customers, employees, suppliers and communities for the immediate return to shareholders ultimately affects the long-term viability of each shareholder's investment. Organizations that fail to do their duty to all groups eventually corrupt their ability to effectively work with any group.

As Allan V. Cecil, P.R. Director of National Gypsum explains, "The main thing was that the company had been saved, jobs and benefits for workers were secure, and shareholders and customers had benefited. In fact, an investor that had purchased a thousand shares of National Gypsum common stock on April 29, 1985 would have seen a 139 percent increase a year later!"

Since that time, a downturn in building starts, coupled with the high cost of borrowed money, has forced National Gypsum Company into chapter eleven. While the eventual outcome remains to be seen, discussions with management at the company indicates they feel this is a liquidity problem and not an ethical problem—and that all creditors and suppliers will be dealt with fairly and equitably.

Do Duties Ever Conflict?

As the previous example shows, doing your duty doesn't always make you popular or guarantee instant success. It does, however, produce positive long term benefits. Earlier we mentioned Howard Putnam and the initial Braniff bankruptcy. The result of Putnam's sense of duty was that Braniff emerged from bankruptcy without a single shareholder lawsuit. On the personal level, former employees were known to still carry handwritten notes received from Putnam years afterwards. Duty may have its costs in the short term, but it reaps incredible rewards over the long haul.

What do you do if you are caught in a situation where, in spite of your efforts to do your duty, you're perceived as derelict? Perhaps just follow the advice of French playwright Pierre Corneille (1606-1684), "Do your duty and leave the rest to heaven."[2]

As leaders we often we have several paths of duty to trod. Those paths may diverge, but we do not believe they have to conflict.

On the surface, there may appear to be a conflict among paths because each group with whom we deal has a different need. On closer examination, however, we usually find that the paths of duty are intertwined, and meeting one need does not necessarily prevent us from meeting another. When Charles E. Wilson, President of General Motors, was nominated by President Eisenhower as Secretary of Defense in 1953, Senator Richard Russell asked him if he would be willing, if necessary, to make a decision unfavorable to General Motors. Wilson said, "What's good for the country is good for General Motors, and vise versa." That is often the way it is with our duties, they are so intertwined and interdependent that whatever helps or hurts one helps or hurts all.

What do shareholders need? A high rate of return on their investment or, failing that, a secure investment.

What do customers need? Good, dependable products and services that offer value.

What do employees need? Secure employment, competitive pay and benefits, a sense of corporate and self worth.

What do suppliers need? They want a customer who pays a fair price on time—who considers them a partner in profit, a member of the team.

What does the community need? They want good corporate citizens who will provide jobs and opportunities for their people as well as expand the tax base so they can afford to provide good schools, streets and services.

As a leader faced with these divergent needs, you can't "do your duty" to any group without doing your duty to the others. If you meet the needs of shareholders but not of employees, you have strikes. If you meet the needs of employees but not shareholders, they dump your stock on the market. If you don't meet the needs of your customers, then everyone is out of a job. Your duty then lies in doing your best for all of them.

The following actions will help you sort out the tough choices that often accompany the challenges of duty:

- **Understand your priorities.** The leaders at the National Gypsum Company defined their first duty as protecting the long-term viability of the company. The leaders at Johnson & Johnson took their duty from their credo. These priorities were determined before a crisis occurred and not in the heat of the moment. By defining their duty in advance, leaders have a point of reference on which to rely when difficult situations arise.

- **Focus on needs rather that wants.** Spencer Johnson, M.D., describes "wants" as those things we wish we could do. "Needs" are the necessities we wish we had done. It is helpful to place ourselves into the future when making a difficult decision Is this an issue of "wants" or "needs"? If we are honoring ourselves and others, we will choose the course of action that allows us to look back on our decision and say, "I did what was right. I did my duty."

- **Understand the needs of others.** Challenges to our sense of duty often involve questions of balancing two rights. For instance, a choice between following a manager's questionable request or resisting can come down to a question of duty to yourself and duty to your family. If you follow the request, you will retain your job, but you will have to live with the feeling that your integrity has been violated. You can maintain your personal honor by refusing to follow the directive, but you might lose your job in the process. Both a duty to self and a duty to family are important. Rather than to jump to an immediate conclusion, it may be helpful to talk with your boss and explain your dilemma. We suggest opening the conversation with something like, "Mary, I have a problem." Then explain your concern in a professional, unemotional manner. Listen to the individual's response and ask questions to determine if there is another way to meet everyone's need without violating your sense of honor and duty. You still might have to take a course of action that puts one of your duties in jeopardy, but at least you will have done your part to understand the situation from the other perspective.

- **Think "and" not "or".** Approaching questions of duty from an "either/or" perspective limits our ability to develop creative solutions that meet everyone's needs. We should never yield on a point of principle, but our experience tells us that people are more likely to limit their options through "either/or" decision making rather than look for ways to expand their options. Remember, honorable people never ask if they should do their duty; they only ask how. Don't rush to close off the options.

- **Have the courage to act.** Leaders willingly take responsibility for their decisions and actions. Their choice may occasionally be unpleasant, but it is made with a clear understanding of the needs of all involved. The honorable leader works to do her duty to everyone concerned.

It is easy to believe that business decisions like the ones made by Johnson & Johnson and the National Gypsum Company are easily made. After all, they are reported so "matter of factly" by the media. Our experience suggests otherwise. The action reported as a company decision was made by individuals with the courage to do their duty. That same courage is required of leaders in all walks of life, as we shall see in the following profile.

LEADERSHIP IN ACTION: DWIGHT D. EISENHOWER

The values and influences that shaped the life of the thirty-fourth President of the United States began October 14, 1890. Dwight David Eisenhower was the third son born to David and Ida Stover Eisenhower. He was born in Denison, Texas, and grew up in Abilene, Kansas. His family, he said later in life, was poor "but the glory of America is that we didn't know it then. All that we knew was that our parents—of great courage—could say to us, 'Opportunity is all about you. Reach out and take it.' "[3]

Eisenhower's sense of duty was no doubt, influenced by his family's deep faith, the mid-America value system of the times, and his military training. Biographer Stephen Ambrose stated in a televised lecture[4] that Eisenhower was only known to have lied twice in his public life. First, to Hitler on the location of the Normandy invasion during World War II; and second, in May 1960, when he lied to Nikita Khreshchev about what Francis Gary Powers was doing in a U–2 spy plane over the Soviet Union. Ambrose states that he never knew him to lie in his private life.

Nowhere was Dwight Eisenhower's sense of duty more distinguished than in his decision to run for President in 1952. He was continuously asked of his intentions, and each time his response was a denial of any such action. Eisenhower did not believe soldiers should be politicians, and he worked to dispel people's growing desire to have the general who defeated Hitler lead the country.

Despite his personal feelings, he acknowledged the one thing that would cause him to enter the political fray—a sense of duty. Eisenhower is quoted as saying, "If I ever do so it will be as the result of a series of circumstances that crush all my arguments, that there appears to me to be such a compelling reason to enter the political field that refusal to do so would always thereafter mean to me that I'd failed to do my duty."[5]

That duty ultimately presented itself. The Republican Party had no sense of leadership at the time. Senator Robert Taft, a leading contender for the nomination, maintained a strong isolationist position that Eisenhower felt would hurt the country in the long run. The other leading Republican voice was Senator Joe McCarthy. Eisenhower, likewise, viewed McCarthy's anti-Communist crusade as disruptive.

He had already severed ties with the Truman Administration over a budget disagreement and had other concerns about the administration's policies. Left with these alternatives, Eisenhower did his duty once again and allowed his name to be entered as a Republican candidate.

Dwight Eisenhower was not a perfect man. His anger was legendary, and his failure to defend his mentor, General George Marshall, when he was being attacked by McCarthy was a mistake that he would later regret.

He was, however, by many estimates a leader of vision, integrity, courage, and character. He knew his constituents, understood their needs, and displayed the courage to act as a leader. Above all else, he did his duty.

Interactive Exercise

The leader who focuses all of his or her attention on only one area risks the disruption of relations with the others. If shareholders and stakeholders are ignored, they will cease to support the organization. If employees are ignored, lower productivity may result. If suppliers are ignored, it becomes difficult to secure the resources the organization needs to operate. If the community is ignored, the loss of support influences all other areas.

Let's assume that you are in charge of a business. What is your "duty" to the following groups, and how would you demonstrate that duty?

Group: Shareholders

Duty:	Action you would take:

Group: Customers

Duty:	Action you would take:

Group: Employees

Duty:	Action you would take:

Group: Suppliers

Duty:	Action you would take:

Group: Community

Duty:	Action you would take:

Duty Calls From Many Directions

In the previous exercise, we looked at our duties to those with whom we work. We have other duties as well. We have duties to our family, our friends, and to ourselves. The balance required of successful leaders extends beyond work into all other areas of life. Without that balance, we lose the perspective that allows us to see the "big picture" of life. The massive generators that supply our electricity have to receive preventive maintenance occasionally. Taking a day off to fish, play golf, have a family outing, or spend time with friends can enable you to "do your duty" more effectively and efficiently.

In the spaces below, write down your duty to those outside the organization and the actions you will take to more effectively live up to that responsibility.

Group: Family

Duty:	Action I will take:

Group: Friends

Duty:	Action I will take:

Group: Myself

Duty:	Action I will take:

A call to duty is not inborn, it is developed. We do our duty, even when we would sometimes rather not, because we have either been trained or have trained ourselves. We do our duty because we are people of honor, committed to succeed and to help others succeed.

Eddie Rickenbacker was a champion auto racer, but when World War I began, his sense of duty caused him to leave that behind and join the Army, where he became America's leading air ace. In 1938, he became President of

Eastern Air Lines. During World War II, he was on an inspection trip for Secretary of War Stimson and was forced down in the Pacific where he drifted on a rubber raft for 24 days before being rescued. After the war, he returned to full-time duties at Eastern, and served as its president until 1959 when he became Chairman of the Board. He did his duty as a young man, as a elderly man, and all the days of his life. Why? Where did he learn his doctrine of duty? The answer may surprise you.

Rickenbacker says, "My first job was as important as any I ever had. It was my initiation into a man's world. Being a newsboy taught me the meaning of duty, and without a sense of duty a man is nothing." Many young people today don't consider a paper route very important—yet one of the greatest men of our time says it was the most important thing in developing his sense of duty. He learned to make commitments and keep them. He learned to depend on himself—and to make himself dependable. The things he learned peddling his papers lasted a lifetime.

Earlier in this chapter, we raised a question, "How can we cultivate a sense of duty in a world where it appears that no one is willing to accept responsibility for anything?" The best way is by our own example, by letting others see how important duty is to us. Duty and responsibility can be learned the way anything is learned: by observation, by study, and by practice. Children learn about duty from teachers, parents, and their peers. The people we lead learn from us. But where do leaders go to learn about duty? Here are a few ideas on how you can enhance your commitment to "do your duty."

- **Find a friend, co-worker, or boss who exhibits a strong sense of duty.** Watch how that individual responds to the challenges of balancing all of life's duties. Ask that individual for feedback when you face the challenges associated with doing your duty.

- **Look for positive examples from history.** Find out all you can about the individual(s) you chose. Establish them as your personal "Board of Advisors," and ask yourself, "How would that person have responded in this situation?"

- **Identify people in your community or your profession to serve as mentors.** Many of the leaders in your community or profession are willing to invest time in people they see are committed to personal improvement and service. However, if you approach one of these people, make certain you are prepared to use their time wisely. They, in all probability, will be giving up something to help you. Make sure their efforts are worthwhile.

- **Put yourself in situations where you must do your duty on a regular basis.** Commit to helping some individual or group. Make a special effort to help someone else learn the importance of doing their duty. Begin talking with others about the importance of duty. Nothing moves us to action like the pressure of knowing others are watching our behavior.

Daniel Webster said, "A sense of duty pursues us ever. It is omnipresent, like the Deity. If we take to ourselves the wings of the morning and dwell in the uttermost parts of the sea, duty performed or duty violated is still with us, for our happiness or our misery. If we say the darkness shall cover us, in the darkness, as in the light our obligations are yet with us."

We do not get to decide whether or not to have duties. Duties come with the territory. Our only choice is how we choose to do our duty. Our professional and our personal lives hang on how wisely we choose. How will you choose?

"ON MY HONOR, I WILL"

In the space provided, list the commitments you wish to make regarding your duty.

NOTES

CHAPTER 5

TO GOD AND MY COUNTRY

A Scout's first duty is to God and country. Our relationship to our God defines our relationship to others, just as our relationship to our country defines the boundaries of our identity and loyalty. When the Scout Oath was written, most Americans had a common concept of God based on Judeo-Christian roots. Beliefs vary, and Scouting takes into account the differences in today's more pluralistic society. Yet, the belief that we are accountable for our actions toward others is a basic religious concept.

Moses handed down the principles of accountability to the children of Israel in the form of the Ten Commandments. Christ proclaimed them to his followers by saying that love for one another was the only way for people to know that they were his disciples. Philosophers and other religious teachers such as Buddha, Confucius, and Aristotle, also, have their teaching grounded in the belief that we are accountable for our actions. This belief is best described in the Golden Rule, "Do unto others as you would have them do unto you."[1] This belief forms the underpinning of integrity and morality in our dealing with others. It is the foundation of our ethical and legal system, for without the concept of "right and wrong" there would be no basis for common guidelines. The belief that lying, cheating, stealing, and murder are morally wrong led to the creation of laws against them.

Some would tell us that such moral underpinnings are out of step with today's society. There are those who act as if they believe that "greed is good," that the Golden Rule should read, "Do unto others before they do unto you" and that you should "look out for number one." Those who follow these principles rarely succeed long-term. Their downfall is based on the short-sighted view that you can continually treat people unfairly and with disrespect and expect them to keep doing business with you.

In truth, the opposite occurs. The long-term successes in business and life follow a moral code defined by the Golden Rule and expanded to recognize that ultimately we all want to be treated as individuals. This code defines people's relationship to their higher calling, whether it be religious or moral, by defining their relationship to others through action.

Likewise, our duty to country provides and identifies a sense of belonging necessary for our survival and success. Technology, cooperation among nations, and world economics have blurred the lines of individual countries. We now operate as a part of the global market, dealing with a number of other trading partners. Technology allows a business in New York to be linked directly and simultaneously with Tokyo, Berlin, Moscow, Mexico City, and Montreal. Yet, a sense of identity and belonging still exists. Travelers worldwide still identify themselves by their country of origin when visiting a foreign nation.

The Boy Scouts, in 1907, saw duty to country as an obligation to fight and protect it from outside aggressors, to vote, serve on juries, take part in the governing process and issues of the day, and to build strong families and communities. Those needs still exist today. In fact, the need has increased. As our country has grown and changed, we have seen example after example of groups and individuals violating its laws and becoming irresponsible in their service. Today, many who are called for jury duty walk into court with every possible excuse not to serve. Others feel compelled to get out of jury duty because their employer doesn't pay them if they are not at work. Many of the same people later bemoan the rise of crime in the streets.

Complaining about the actions of our elected leaders has become a national pastime, but voter apathy remains high. The list could go on and on of people showing disrespect for their duty to their country and complaining because things are not going as they would have them.

If we thumb our noses at our moral duty to others and our duty to country, we should not be surprised by people around us not meeting theirs. Society's norms are established by individuals like us getting involved. C.S. Lewis observed, "We laugh at honor and are surprised to find there are traitors in our midst." The many treason cases that have come to light would indicate that Professor Lewis was right. But more importantly, Lewis was telling us that unless individual people become active in fulfilling their duty to God and country, we should not be surprised when our country and its people do not make good decisions and maintain moral behavior. The bad examples are well reported in the press. Fortunately, there is no shortage of good examples of organizations and leaders who honor their God and their country, and by doing so, achieve greater success. Let's look at some of them.

LEADERSHIP IN ACTION: W.W. "FOOTS" CLEMENTS

W.W. "Foots" Clements, Chairman Emeritus of the Dr Pepper Company, learned the value of honor and commitment to God and country at home and as a Boy Scout. Growing up in rural Alabama, he learned to pull his weight at an early age. His first job was carrying lunches to farm workers, and when he was big enough, he tended turkeys, chopped weeds, and hoed cotton. His first work "for pay" was trapping opossums, selling their skins for $1.25. When he was eleven, he took a weekend job working in a combination grocery store and gristmill. As he grew older, he hauled lumber, ran a newspaper route, and sold magazines. By the time he was in high school, he was working as a part-time butcher.

In 1935, at the age of 21, "Foots" took a job as a route salesman for the Dr Pepper Bottling Company in Tuscaloosa, Alabama at $10 a week. In 1942, he was hired by the Dr Pepper Company itself as a zone manager. By 1967, he was Executive Vice President and a director. Two years later, he became President and Chief Operating Officer, and CEO the following year. In 1980, he became Chairman of the Board, becoming Chairman Emeritus in 1986.

During Clements' years at the helm of Dr Pepper, he was able to transform this small, regional soft drink into the number three soft drink in America. While this kind of drive and determination would consume all the resources of most men, Clements accomplished it in addition to a full load in a host of civic and outside business responsibilities. He served as a director of banks, life insurance companies, colleges, hospitals, and such organizations as the Laymen's National Bible Committee, Better Business Bureau, American Red Cross, The Salvation Army, U.S.O., and the Circle Ten Council of The Boy Scouts, to name a few. Asked if he ever got tired, he laughed, "Sure, there has been a lifetime of long days and long weeks. But, the things I did for God, and country, and community made me a better person. Everything I did ultimately helped me in my job." W.W. Clements not only has a Horatio Alger success story, he is a recipient of the Horatio Alger award for his "boot strap" rise from poverty to success.

"Foots" has given away thousands of marbles with the Golden Rule written on them. Skeptics ask, "Can you build a competitive business on the Golden Rule?" He always answers, "You cannot build a business that will last except by practicing the Golden Rule. Our people at Dr Pepper are taught this. It is our foundation." "Foots" feels that if you have ability and follow the Golden Rule, you'll succeed. As he told the students at Tuscaloosa County High School on Horatio Alger Day on March 6, 1990, "Horatio Alger members are people who recognize and understand that you can't do it alone...we are motivated to put something back into the system that has been so good to us—not just our money, but our time and effort to help others understand the abundant opportunities that exist in our country...I hope you will be convinced that if I made it, anyone can make it if they work hard and follow the Golden Rule."

LEADERSHIP IN ACTION: GERBER BABY FOODS

On July 28, 1990, the Associated Press ran the following story:

Raymond Dunn, Jr., turned 16 Tuesday, but the profoundly retarded birthday boy feasted not on cake, to which he is allergic, but on the day's greatest gift: the bland, brown infant formula that keeps him alive.

Gerber Products Co., which stopped making the meat-based formula in 1985, resumed production two months ago after Raymond's doctors said that he would die without it. Gerber employees volunteered to make a batch on their own time, and on June 26 the Dunn's received a two-year supply free of charge.

"Gerber says, 'Babies are our business,' but Raymond is their business too," said Carol Dunn, who spent five years trying to get the company to retool for a market of one. When Gerber decided to drop the product five years ago, Mrs. Dunn was unable to find or create any substitute that did not make Raymond sick. Frantic, she hunted down every can she could find, and Gerber kept passing along its own backlog. By July, 1988, Gerber ran out of MBF, leaving Raymond with less than two year's supply.

Supported by the State Association for Retarded Children, Mrs. Dunn begged Gerber to make more MBF, and began a mail campaign asking others to pressure the company. Finally, the company's research director consented. Meanwhile, at Gerber, volunteers in the research division put their own projects on hold, hauled out old equipment, and devoted several thousand square feet and several days of production space and time to Raymond's supply of MBF. It arrived in Yankee Lake (NY) in time. The Dunn's had about two dozen cans of the old formula, enough to last through the end of July.

Why would a company and its employees go to so much trouble for a market of one? The obvious answer was that they really cared. To skeptics that might counter with, "But, they got a lot of good publicity out of it!" we respond, "So? What's wrong with getting credit for a good deed?"

Why Do We Do What We Do?

As "Foots" Clements observed, "Not only do we have a responsibility to our business, our employees, and the people we serve, but also to our system, our home and to God." Our responsibility to a higher calling, be it religious or moral, assumes that the actions we take to help others are taken because we want to, not because we have to or expect recognition.

Truly successful people, leaders, and organizations recognize this and act accordingly. Their decision to give back to society and practice the Golden Rule is based on an internal motivation. They expect little in return except the satisfaction of seeing others have the opportunity to experience success. In the Old Testament story, Cain asked God, "Am I my brother's keeper?[2]" The answer was, "Yes!" We all have a responsibility to be involved in the social issues of our day. It makes for good business because it make for good people.

LEADERSHIP IN ACTION: GOLDEN RULE LIFE INSURANCE COMPANY

Golden Rule Life Insurance Company began in 1940 with a pledge to follow the Golden Rule in all their business dealings. Today, they have $5.9 billion of insurance in force and premium income for 1990 was $450,000,000. We asked Richard Merrill, Vice President of Financial Products, if the company was committed to that rule regardless of the consequences. He laughed and said, "Of course we are."

Pressed for an example, he said, "Shortly after I came here in 1984, we were marketing a single premium whole life product which offered unusual advantages for the clients of insurance brokers. Prior to changes in the tax law in 1988, insurance companies had almost $40 billion worth of this product in force."

"Even though we were early into the market and had a chance to capture a major market share, our products had one distinction from the others. The competitors' products advertised their policy as having "no insurance charges" which meant if you put $25,000 into the policy, the computer illustration showed money growing, for example, at a net 9 percent interest rate with no charges against it."

"By contrast, our product showed a 10 percent interest rate and an insurance charge of 1 percent. Although the bottom line return to the customer was the same, we felt telling the whole truth made it clear that the customer was paying for insurance. We felt this was important; because as people get older, the insurance charges increase, and we wanted people to understand this fully going in."

Merrill added, "I have to admit as a product manager whose bonus was based on production, my natural inclination was to join the herd and do it the way everyone else did. I spoke to our CEO, J. Patrick Rooney, about it, and he was adamant that we follow the Golden Rule. He merely pointed to the company's mission statement that says:

> **'At Golden Rule, we choose to be ethical because it is right, not because it is good business practice. We value hard work and promptness, and we are committed to doing things right. We want our products to provide our customers with the best long-term value in the marketplace.'**

"As a result, our sales were sluggish—so there was a very big price to pay for doing the right thing. However, a change in the tax law eventually killed the product line for everyone. When that happened, nearly all our competitors decreased the interest rate credited to the policies to offset the hidden insurance costs. Today, a lot of our business comes from customers of those policies who liked our "tell it like it is" approach, plus quite a few who bought competitors' products and found it was really as we said it was. So, in the long run, doing the honorable thing, the right thing and, following the Golden Rule, pays off."

We Are Accountable To Country

In his inaugural address, President John F. Kennedy observed, "To whom much is given, much is required. And when at some future date the high court of history sits in judgment on each of us, recording whether in our brief span of service we fulfilled our responsibilities to the state, our success or failure, in whatever office we hold, will be measured by the answers to four questions: First, were we truly men of courage? Second, were we truly men of judgment? Third, were we truly men of integrity? Finally, were we truly men of dedication?"

Noble words for a President, but what do they mean for those of us who are just "average citizens?" How do we "do our duty" to our country? One way is active participation.

Our duty to country includes:

- **Paying our taxes**
- **Serving on juries**
- **Obeying the laws**
- **Voting**
- **Involvement in schools, education and social issues**
- **Serving in the armed forces when necessary**
- **Involvement in building strong families and communities**

In a very real sense, doing our duty to our country is doing our duty to ourselves. Since our country provides us with safety and security, doing our duty is in our own best interest. We must help the "ship of state" sail on, because if the ship sinks, all the passengers are in peril.

The day after World War II began, Melvin Baker, President of National Gypsum Company, sent a telegram to War Secretary Henry Stimson that said, "The management of this corporation believes that business should go all out for quick, decisive victor…and to this end, the company's resources, technical knowledge and the production at its twenty-one plants are at your disposal." The government was quick to take Baker up on the offer and sent a team of attorneys to work out the details with the company's attorneys. As the haggling over the details dragged on, Baker stood up and said, "There's a war on. Let's forget about dotting the 'i's'. We're in this thing together!" Both sets of attorneys were startled into silence for a moment, then they laughed and quickly signed the necessary papers.

Baker's statement is still appropriate today. We are engaged in a war, fighting such enemies as homelessness, poverty, hunger, illiteracy, discrimination, substance addiction, and a host of other problems that threaten to sink the "ship of state". Our duty to country is a duty to ourselves. Ultimately, everyone's interest is best served when the needs of each individual are met.

My Country and the World

Today, we live in a global village, and we must both co-exist and compete with the world. An individual's first responsibility is to family and friends, then to his or her own community and country. However, responsibility must extend to the rest of the world. As fellow travelers on spaceship Earth, we share a common destiny, just as if we were passengers on the same steamship. If the front of a ship sinks, the back follows. If the front of a ship sails safely into port, the back does, too.

John Donne, in his book *Devotions Upon Emergent Occasions,* written in 1624, perhaps said it best:

No man is an island, entire of itself; every man is a piece of the continent, a part of the main; if a clod be washed away by the sea, Europe is the less, as well as if a promontory were, as well as if a manor of thy friends or of thine own were; any man's death diminishes me, because I am involved in mankind; and therefore never send to know for whom the bell tolls; it tolls for thee.

It is easy to take the advantage of country for granted. Sometimes the spectacular can become almost commonplace, and it is only when we return after a long absence that we can really understand what country means to us. Sometimes, it is easier to see it through the eyes of another.

When Hue Cao fled Vietnam with her mother and two brothers in 1979, she spoke no English. Yet, in 1986, she won a state-sponsored essay contest on "What the Statue of Liberty Means to Me." Her essay said, in part, "We wanted to live in America, a land where there is liberty and justice. Every time we saw a picture of the Statue of Liberty, my mother would tell us *she* is America. America is a place that lends a hand to those in need. The Americans care for all people, from hopeless to homeless."

There is a lot of truth in Hue Cao's words—Americans care. No country has ever approached the generosity of America. No nation in history has matched us in either total or per capita giving. We give as individuals. We give as corporations. We give as a country. Caring and sharing are part of our national heritage. It was a major factor in the survival of the early settlers, and it must continue today both here and abroad.

It is easy to feel hopeless about the challenges that exist in the world. There are so many staggering needs. Many feel that there is little use. After all, what can one person do?

Syndicated columnist George Will says, "Over and over, we hear people ask, 'What can I do—I'm only one person?' That's a non-question, since you can never be more than one person!" None of us are able to do everything, but each of us is able to do something to make this a better world. It is our duty. C.S. Lewis wrote, "We have no right to happiness. We have only an obligation to do our duty." Writer Cal Thomas says, "It is in doing that duty that ultimate happiness is to be found." History tells us that it is often a mistake to underestimate the power of one individual committed to a leadership based on commitment to God and country. Our next case study is an excellent example of what we mean.

LEADERSHIP IN ACTION: ORRIN HATCH

The March 17, 1995 edition of *USA Today* ran the following headline on page 8A: "Sen. Hatch, marching to his own drummer—Utah Conservative guided by 'what's right,' not party politics." On one hand, we find it interesting that the writers thought a public servant committed to do what is right an oddity. On the other hand, we applaud them for showing us a glimpse at the life of a leader who uses his personal faith and duty to country as a guide for his own actions without using it as a tool to berate the behavior of others.

That some people consider Hatch to be the "conservative's conservative" is no secret. He went about doing his duty largely unnoticed by the public outside his home state of Utah, until the Clarence Thomas Supreme Court confirmation hearing. His performance there angered many liberals. The true example of Hatch's commitment to doing what is right, we believe, can be found in the decisions he has made that stand in contrast to the party line. The Senator from Utah has come out against term limits and for child care. He, according to the *USA Today* article, "champions nutrition programs for the poor, AIDS education, more money for research on breast cancer and immunizing children." His beliefs have made him something of a dissident in his own party on more than one occasion.

What drives Orrin Hatch? We only need to look at his own statements and life. He has been quoted saying,. "I am a strong believer in Jesus Christ and his principles. Am I perfect? No. But I work on it all the time. I try to do what's right." His faith is a guide in his life, and as a result he strives to do what's right. Senator Hatch understands that his commitment will occasionally make people angry. Nevertheless, he counts a diverse group of individuals as friends, most notably, ex-boxer Muhammed Ali, novelist Patricia Cornwell, actress Victoria Principal, and Senator

Edward Kennedy, a man considered by many to be the liberal's liberal.

A strong personal faith is a common factor among many successful leaders, including those profiled here. Zig Ziglar cited an April 28, 1986 *Fortune* magazine article in the foreword of this book. It says that 91 percent of Fortune 500 CEOs are people of faith. The majority of these leaders never publicize their faith through words. Instead, they rely on their beliefs in duty to God and country to guide their choices and actions. They understand the ultimate example of duty is our willingness to honor our beliefs when faced with difficult decisions.

The pace of change is more rapid now than at any time in our history. Technological, political, and economic shifts are occurring today that will forever influence our ability to respond as individuals and organizations. Businesses are facing pressures from global competition. Individuals and families face pressures from societal changes in the way we look at life, work, and relationships. In all cases, a strong understanding of our faith, our relationships to others, our identity, and our loyalties provides an anchor that steadies us in turbulent waters.

For those looking for good news, we offer several rays of hope. We are more likely than ever before to find individuals and organizations taking the lead in doing what is right for everyone. We have seen global cooperation on whaling, acid rain, ozone depletion, reduction of the rain forests, and in quarantining aggressor nations. As more and more people, organizations, and countries come to realize that we are all passengers on the same ship, we can expect to see more and more who are willing to work together to "do their duty" in the future.

Whether it is leading to clean up pollution, provide educational opportunities for those poorly served by the system, ensure food and shelter for the homeless, or one of many other "causes" that deserve attention, our duty is the same—to give back and to follow the Golden Rule in all our actions.

"ON MY HONOR, I WILL"

In the space provided, list the commitments you wish to make to follow the Golden Rule and give back to society.

NOTES

CHAPTER 6

TO OBEY THE SCOUT LAW

Laws are the rules and regulations that enable us to live together in harmony and peace. They are also the guidelines and principles that, if followed, will produce consistent results.

The average person, for instance, looks at laws as the rules by which we should live. They look at the 55 MPH speed limit on non-interstate U.S. highways as a rule that governs the way they drive. They view the laws regarding personal conduct as the boundaries by which people everywhere live in harmony. Robert Frost said, "Good fences make good neighbors." Laws, if you will, are the "good fences" that separate our rights from our neighbor's rights and permit us all to live in relative harmony. Laws in societies everywhere establish the foundation for those society's' actions.

In a simpler time, people followed the principles embodied in the Scout Law without questioning why. Those few people who didn't were ostracized, or at least held in contempt. But, those days are gone, and times today are different and more complex. Today, we sometimes see those who violate the principles of integrity honored as if bad were good and right were wrong. When we see such things, it's logical to ask, "Why would anyone in today's competitive environment want to follow such strong principles?" It's a good question, and fortunately, there's a good answer. Leaders of integrity know that by following these principles, they will reap multiplied results for themselves and their organizations. In return for their efforts as managers, they receive results such as:

- **Increased loyalty from employees and customers**
- **Word-of-mouth advertising**
- **Fewer people problems**
- **Safer work environments**
- **Increased profits**
- **Less personal stress**
- **Increased personal satisfaction and perspective**

In return for their efforts as individuals, they receive results such as:

- **Increased trust from the important people in their lives**
- **Respect of others**
- **A feeling of faith, hope, and optimism that fills their lives**
- **Security in themselves and their relationships**
- **Improved relationships and communication with others**

- **Confidence in their ability to withstand the challenges that present themselves**

It almost sounds too easy, doesn't it? Obey a few principles that have been around forever and reap incredible results. Conventional wisdom tells us that anything that sounds too good to be true probably is too good to be true. Are we countering conventional wisdom? Absolutely not.

Like the Ten Commandments, the Magna Carta, and the Bill of Rights, which forms the first ten amendments of the U.S. Constitution, the Scout Law is based on principles that work. Many good examples are given in this book— hundreds more could be given. The principle is that you reap what you sow. It applies to every life, every business, every industry. What goes in will, in time, come out— multiplied.

The Story of XYZ Manufacturing

Several years ago a Midwest manufacturing company decided to implement a "Values Program." The program's stated purpose was to send a clear message to customers, employees, suppliers, and the community that XYZ Manufacturing was trustworthy. The senior management team knew and believed that the company's image among customers, suppliers, and the community depended on the behavior of the organization's employees. The senior managers also knew that their trust, loyalty, respect, and credibility were in short supply with employees. Years before, there had been a bitter strike, and the wounds had never completely healed. Employees felt betrayed and mistreated. Their feelings were transmitted to the community and to customers.

XYZ management adopted several strategies to implement their "Values Program." They posted plaques, printed cards for wallets, and created stickers for hard hats. They mailed letters to every home, and placed value-oriented articles in all the local papers. "Values" was the subject of every speech and every company newsletter. Everything that could be done to carry out the new "Values Program" was done, except one—managers did not change the way they managed.

XYZ forgot the basic premise of change: *the main thing is to make the main thing the main thing.* They were trying to put a bandage on a cancer and overcome 50 years of problems with a public relations campaign. Management wasn't trying to "pull a fast one." They honestly believed that a few plaques, cards, decals, letters, speeches, and articles would make a difference! They wanted the results without paying the price. They wanted to give lip service to the law of reciprocity without actually living the law.

Was XYZ's "Values Program" another example of "management-by-best-seller"? Unfortunately the answer is yes—but it didn't have to be. Most strategic initiatives, management development programs, and cultural change projects adopted by organizations today are philosophically sound and well-intentioned. The challenge lies in getting people at all levels of the organization to admit that change does need to occur and that it must begin with them. In the case of XYZ Manufacturing, the only way to convince workers that management's intent was honorable would have been for everyone from the CEO on down to admit they had done wrong and wanted to improve. Nothing less than total candor, total commitment, and total change would have sufficed.

The same is true in our personal lives as well. We assume that stating our intentions in our own "P.R." campaign will convince others that we are serious about changing our lives. For instance, the membership rolls at local health clubs swell at the beginning of each new year as people announce their intention to get in shape. It is even difficult to find a parking space for a few weeks as the use of the facilities increases. The serious members know that they must wait it out until the intentions wear off. Within a month, things are usually back to normal. We may judge ourselves by our intentions, but others judge us by our actions over time.

Emerson put it this way, "What you are stands over you the while, and thunders so that I cannot hear what you say to the contrary."[1] Leaders with integrity commit themselves over time to live principles every day. They know that living these natural laws is more important than talking about them.

That said, let's look more closely at the principles contained in the Boy Scout Law. The original words of the law are in large, bold type. Our commentary follows.

The Scout Law

A Scout is:

Trustworthy. Trust is the basis for all successful relationships. Without trust, people do not feel free to look at options for mutual success, and believability diminishes. You can count on trustworthy leaders to focus on what's right rather than who's right, to be consistent in their dealings with people and to be honest. The most important task of leadership in changing times is to build trust. It is accomplished by being trustworthy in our character, competence, and consistency of action.

Loyal. In the past, loyalty was a "given." Loyalty to employees, employers, customers, and business associates has diminished as the focus of business and life has turned toward immediate rather than long-term satisfaction. An article in the November 8, 1990, *USA Today* pointedly demonstrates how loyalty has changed. A 1925 list created by Boston University School of Management Professor Fred Foulkes, cited 30 U.S. firms with "no layoff" practices. The article reported that the list had diminished to eight companies. Loyalty does not mean that a leader or an organization will never have to deal with unpleasant issues like layoffs or restructuring. The loyal leader, however, looks for creative ways to help those they lead meet their goals. Leading with integrity requires us to be loyal to those individuals and groups on whom we depend and who depend on us.

Helpful. Zig Ziglar says, "You can get everything in life you want if you'll help enough other people get what they want." In other words, being helpful pays dividends. The dividends occur in two ways. First, you receive an internal dividend. That dividend comes in the good feeling you get when you realize that you have assisted someone in reaching a goal or solving a problem. The satisfaction alone makes helping worthwhile. Second, you receive an external dividend. It comes from the reciprocity you receive when you help others. Helping others creates an atmosphere of trust and loyalty that results in people helping you.

Friendly. Leaders may be given the right to lead, but they earn the right to be followed. Being friendly communicates a humanness that commands respect. Friendliness doesn't have to mean being best friends. It does mean acknowledging people as individuals with their own special personalities and likes.

Courteous. The root of courtesy is respect. The leader with integrity respects the opinions, beliefs, customs and values of others. He or she encourages individuals to state their opinions and then listens. He or she respects beliefs and values and doesn't impose his own morals on others, choosing instead to let his behavior speak for him. It's easy to limit courtesy to holding the door open for others and saying please and thank you. The leader who practices courtesy does these things and more, continually looking for ways to make the people around him feel important.

Kind. Leaders who lead with integrity have a high self-esteem. They have no need to make others look bad in order to make themselves look better. They demonstrate their self-esteem through kindness. Kindness is not the same as being unwilling to say something bad to someone. Kindness means that we design an approach that enables people to preserve their dignity and help them improve. Mary Kay Ash, founder of Mary Kay Cosmetics, puts it this way, "Whenever I have to talk with someone about a problem, I always want them to feel appreciated for who they are." Howard Putnam, former CEO of Southwest and Braniff Airlines, says that he uses the practice of "getting mad at the problem, not at the person" to keep him on the right track.

Obedient. We often interpret obedience as compliance with the rules and the opposite of what it takes to succeed in today's business environment. Obedience can be positive however. The Boy Scout definition of obedient brings to mind words such as *loyal*, *faithful*, *devoted*, *conforming*, and *law-abiding*. The individual who leads with integrity is obedient to the rules of the organization as well as to his or her own code of honor. Most important, he or she is obedient to the natural laws described here. This type of leader looks for self-evident truths and consistently works to incorporate his into their daily behavior

Cheerful. The Book of Proverbs says, effectively, "a cheerful heart is good medicine."[2] The medicine works for you and all those around you. Scientific evidence points to the fact that the individual who is cheerful experiences less stress and has better health than those who continually worry. Common sense and experience tells us that, all things being equal, people prefer to be around other people who have a cheerful outlook. For the leader in today's changing world, having people who will follow is no guarantee. Being a cheerful leader can help make your organization a place where people want to work.

Thrifty. Leaders understand that success is based on what they keep, not what they make. Thrifty leaders are willing to spend money, to achieve a goal, but as Roy Christensen of the Black Mountain Spring Water Company says, "We try to make our dimes work like dollars."

Brave. Historically, bravery is thought of in the physical sense. Today, bravery most often applies to the courage to follow your dreams and convictions. It is tempting to sacrifice aspirations and principles on the altar of expediency. Sticking to your goal and your principles is just as scary as physical dangers.

Clean. A former tennis coach of Randy's had a saying that describes the importance of a clean body, mind and spirit. "If you look sharp, you feel sharp. If you feel sharp, you act sharp. If you act sharp, you play sharp. If you play sharp, you are sharp." Does appearance have a bearing on success? The answer from two perspectives is yes. First, there is the feeling of self-confidence that comes from looking and feeling your best. Most people can remember the feeling they had when they looked and felt their best. Second, the perceptions we create influence our success. Walk into a luxury store in the clothes normally reserved for painting your home and see how they treat you. Walk in the same store one week later looking your best. Were you treated differently? Hopefully not, but if we were betting people, we'd lay you two to one that you were. Appearance does make a difference.

Reverent. Reverence is a word related to "awe." We should never lose our awe of our creator, of creation, or of human potential. Individuals who respect themselves and command the respect of others have a deep sense of reverence that runs deep and still like a mighty river.

The Scout Law in Action

Have you seen the Scout Law in action lately? Our research shows that there are a literally hundreds of businesses and business people who actively live the Scout Law. Nearly every individual and company represented as a case study in this book is a good example, and we've sprinkled in enough bad examples to show what happens when the proper principles of honor and integrity are ignored. Robert Levering, Milton Moskowitz, and Michael Katz provide a good sampling of executives and organizations who uphold a high level of integrity in their book *The 100 Best Companies to Work for in America* (Addison Wesley, 1984). *Fortune's* annual survey of the "Most Admired Companies" is another good resource, as is *Inc.* magazine and *Forbes*. The key point to remember is that most successful businesses and business people use high principles to guide their daily decisions and actions. You probably won't hear about them in the media because their stories don't make the kind of scintillating copy that draws readers and viewers. Here are a few more examples of how organizations and individuals use integrity to guide their actions and decisions.

Max DePree and Herman Miller, Inc. Herman Miller is the innovative leader of the furniture industry. In 1989, they ranked ninth in *Fortune's* listing of the one of the hundred best companies to work for in the United States. Herman Miller has a history of sharing the company's financial gains with all employees. While businesses everywhere were handing out golden parachutes to executives, Herman Miller was structuring silver parachutes for all employees with over two years of service.

Their actions are motivated by a simple belief in integrity. CEO Max DePree defines integrity as "a fine sense of one's obligations." It is a value handed down from his father, D.J. DePree.

Their organizational and individual integrity is displayed in many small ways ranging from a dedication to superior design, quality products, a commitment to contributing to society, and most important, in its respect for customers, suppliers, employees, and investors.

Max DePree says, "In addition to all the ratios and goals and parameters and bottom lines, it is fundamental that leaders endorse a concept of persons."[3] He believes that "the first responsibility of a leader is to define reality. The last is to say thank you. In between the two, the leaders must become a servant and a debtor."[4]

The results speak for themselves. A hundred dollars invested in Herman Miller in 1975 would have grown at a compounded annual rate of growth of 41 percent by 1986. For those not mathematically inclined, that initial investment would have grown to $4,854.60 in eleven years.[5]

Volvo Cars of North America. Long recognized as one of the safest cars on the road, Volvo showed its integrity with the pulling of its controversial "Monster Truck" ad in the fall of 1990. The ad showed a large truck running over a line of cars—and only the Volvo survived uncrushed. Later, they and everyone else discovered that the ad agency had reinforced the Volvo, not because it wasn't strong enough, but simply so they could video tape it several times without replacing the vehicle. Volvo was innocent of the act, yet they not only pulled the ad, they published a letter of apology and explanation.

The Procter & Gamble Company. Procter & Gamble has a long history of commitment to quality products. Its brands include Pampers, Tide, Charmin, Bounty, Cheer, Cascade, Comet, Sure, and Scope. Most of us have used one or more P&G products. Less well known is P&G's commitment to quality benefits for its people. In 1885, when American workers expected a six-day workweek, P&G began giving employees Saturday afternoon off, with pay. In 1887, they started the first profit-sharing plan in the industry. In 1915, they became one of the first companies in the country to adopt health,[6] disability and life insurance programs for their employees.

Earlier we reported that the list of companies committed to no layoff policies dropped from 30 to 8! P&G is one of those remaining. It began guaranteeing employees at least 48 weeks work each year back in 1923! Today, P&G is pioneering in employee benefits again by offering adoption aid benefits.

Hewlett-Packard Company. Hewlett-Packard is on virtually everyone's "best list," with good reason. H-P has provided a model for growing a successful business and maintaining excellent relationships with customers, suppliers, employees, and the community at large. The company maintains a highly competitive compensation and benefits package. They provide recreation areas for employees, and they remain committed to a tradition of full employment. The company's philosophy, articulated in "The H-P Way," stresses belief in people, respect, dignity, recognition, security, open communication, and a chance to learn and grow. David Packard, one of the founders, as early as 1949, began articulating his philosophy that companies have obligations beyond just making a profit as early at 1949.[7] The words sounded good even then—and have been proven out in practice.

Merck & Company. Merck is one of the most successful pharmaceutical companies in the world, consistently ranking high on everyone's list of most admired companies. Like every major corporation listed here, it is a great place to work. Merck offers great benefits, open communication, challenging and important work, and a strong devotion to maintaining employee morale. But the main reason we included them here is because of a drug called Mectizan. The average person probably knows very little about this drug. It is a cure for "river blindness," a disease that was infecting over a million people in Third World countries. The "problem" with Mectizan was not its ability to cure sickness. It was in the ability for those in need to pay. Many companies for would have abandoned the project all together, but Merck developed it anyway. In the end, Merck gave it all away free to those in need.

George Merck II defined the company's mission as "preserving and improving life." They had proven their commitment by taking streptomycin to Japan after World War II. Their actions made no money, but the Japanese were able to eliminate tuberculosis. When leaders are willing to live by principles, even in the face of no profit, it is easy to understand how they earn the trust, loyalty, and commitment of others.

Black Mountain Spring Water Company. Integrity is especially important to smaller companies. Their reputation depends on it. Black Mountain Spring Water Company believes that its integrity is demonstrated by its service. To make sure that integrity is maintained, the company limited its geographic growth in 1989. According to Roy Christensen, Vice President of Marketing and Operations, and Steve Block, Vice President of Sales, "To provide the kind of service we promised our customers, we had no other choice. A company of integrity can never promise more than they can produce."

Samsonite Corporation. Samsonite Corporation was founded in 1910 by Jesse Shwayder with his life savings ($3500) and a firm conviction that the Golden Rule, "Do unto others as you would have them do unto you," was the only way to do business. Jesse felt what he would have from others was strong luggage—luggage as strong as Samson in the Bible. Samson was the first name of Shwayder's products, and it later became Samsonite—a brand known and recognized for quality around the world. Through all the years, however, the company's adherence to the Golden Rule never varied. Each new employee is given a Golden Rule marble (Samsonite provides the marbles Mary Kay Ash and "Foots" Clements give away) to remind them of the company's philosophy. Samsonite has pioneered many firsts in luggage—first to use vinyl, first to promote fashion colors, first to use ABS and magnesium, first to use hidden locks—yet the basic principle of following the Golden Rule in relations with customers, suppliers, and employees has never changed.

LEADERSHIP IN ACTION: BEN COHEN AND JERRY GREENFIELD

When best friends Ben Cohen and Jerry Greenfield decided they'd like to be in the ice-cream business, they took a $5 ice-cream correspondence course. Armed with all the knowledge $5 could buy and a $12,000 total investment, they developed their own recipes and opened a twelve-flavor ice cream parlor in 1978. Sales are in excess of $100 million a year and Ben & Jerry's is a household name among premium ice cream connoisseurs.

When entrepreneurs start small and grow to gigantic proportions, there's a great temptation to keep all the profits for themselves—after all, there's no legal law against it. Ben Cohen and Jerry Greenfield felt there was a moral law prohibiting them from "taking the money and running." From the very beginning, they became a people-oriented company. For them "people" includes customers, shareholders, employees, and even those who have never heard of Ben & Jerry's Ice Cream. To customers, they provide delicious, homemade-type ice cream. To shareholders, they provide a place for their investment to grow. To employees, they provide free ice cream, free health club memberships to work it off, inexpensive day care, and dependable employment in a family atmosphere. To the people of their communities, Ben & Jerry's provides free ice cream for charitable fund raisers. They set aside seven-and-a-half percent of their pre-tax profits to go to a nonprofit foundation. In spite of the calorie count of their product, there are no "fat cats" at Ben and Jerry's. The health club membership is one reason. Another is that company policy dictated for many years that no executive (including Ben and Jerry) could earn more than five times the salary of the lowest-paid staffer! That ratio was increased to seven in 1990, and the company decided to go beyond that amount when the recruited their new CEO. The real message of Ben & Jerry's is their commitment to continuously improve. For like any start-up business that undergoes rapid growth, there have been missteps along the way.

Fred "Chico" Lager, former Ben & Jerry's CEO, cites a time in 1987 when "most employees would probably not have characterized their day-to-day work as fun."[8] Building a small company that is grappling with explosive growth is demanding—both mentally and physically. *Inc.* magazine described the challenge of remaining true to one's principles of social responsibility and the need to make a profit. Ben, Jerry, and other leaders responded by listening, communicating, and taking action consistent with the laws of being trustworthy and honest. Efforts were made to fix those physical, systematic, direction, and relationship-oriented things that were in need of repair. "Chico" Lager says, "Most of the people who worked at Ben & Jerry's were willing to accept that things were less that perfect, as long as they knew we were aware of what the problems were, and perceived that we were trying to fix them."[9]

Tom Melohn, President of North American Tool and Die, Inc., agrees that the behavior of the leader influences his relationship with others. He says, "If you belong to three country clubs and employ a private secretary, genuine communication with workers could be tough. Those trappings of power say one thing: 'I am better than you.' "

What kind of company have Ben and Jerry built? One staffed by people who are trustworthy, loyal, helpful, friendly, courteous, kind, obedient, cheerful, thrifty, brave, clean, and reverent—the kind of people who obey both legal and moral laws because they're the thing to do, not just because they're afraid of the consequences.

The Best Traits of a Leader

One executive we know says, "The two most important traits for any leader is truthfulness and fairness. The quality of the leader influences the quality of the product. As leaders, we must remember that employees and customers feel, 'When the CEO lies to you, the company lies to you!' "

Good images, like good buildings, take time to construct and often must be built brick-by-brick. Public relations can give your corporate image a boost, but you can't build an image with P.R. Every employee is your image—and they depend on management to set the example. As a leader, you serve as role model for others.

The December 4, 1989 issue of *Fortune* carried an article by Alan Farnham titled, "The Trust Gap." In this article, Farnham says, "Corporate America is split by a gulf between top management and everybody else—in pay, in perks, in self-importance." His point was that it is difficult for a line worker to feel "we're in this together" because workers rightly perceive that management has no concept of what it's like to work in the lower stratas of the business.

The same article mentioned how some companies have worked to solve the problem. Hyatt Hotels sent the entire headquarters staff to work for a day changing sheets, pouring coffee, and running elevators. President Darryl Hartley-Leonard worked as a doorman for a day, alongside Bill Kurvers, full-time door captain. At first the president refused tips, but the other doormen soon set him straight. Farnham asks, "What did he get from his experience, besides tips?" Kurvers says, "He got respect."

The same article reported that Southwest Airlines President Herb Kelleher and other officers work at least once a quarter as baggage handlers, ticket agents, and flight attendants. Kelleher said, "We're trying to create an understanding of the difficulties every person has on his job. When you're actually dealing with customers, and you're doing the job yourself, you're in a better position to appraise the effect of some new program or policy."

The American Indians used to say, "Judge no man until you have walked a mile in his moccasins." Walking with those we lead gives insight into their needs, wants, and feelings. It creates a bonding, a mutual respect that builds and grows. In the Declaration of Independence, the founders of the United States wrote, "We hold these truths to be self-evident, that all men are created equal." If we really believe that, then we'll treat all as equals. This doesn't mean that the janitor in the building makes as much money as the president of the company, but it does mean that we treat the janitor with as much dignity. That is the essence of honoring the laws of being helpful, friendly, courteous, and kind.

The bottom line is that no one cares how much you know about them until they know how much you care about them. As Hyatt's Hartley-Leonard says of his experience, "Employees do feel they're living in a society of equals." How much difference does it make for others to know that their leaders consider them as equals? Successful individuals and organizations everywhere will tell you it makes all the difference in the world.

In the last century, Father Joseph Damien De Veuster left Belgium to devote his life to caring for the lepers on the island of Molokai, Hawaii. For many years, he preached, taught, and cared for these people, but he won few converts to his religion. Then, one morning as he was dressing he noticed a leprous patch on his own skin. He began his mass that day with the words, "My fellow lepers"—and for the first time, those in the leper colony began to really listen to what the priest had to say. His statue represents Hawaii in the United States Capitol in Washington, D.C.

The Scout Law—How to Know it When You See it

We've shared a number of business examples of the Scout Law in action, but our list is neither definitive, nor exhaustive. You probably know other individuals and organizations, many right in your own community that exhibit these principles. You can identify them by answering the following questions.

- **What individuals and organizations come to mind when you think of trust?**

Business/business leaders you trust:	Why do you trust them?

- **What individuals and organizations come to mind when you think of being helpful, friendly, courteous, and kind?**

Names:	Why do you rate them so highly?

- **What individuals and organizations come to mind when you think of being honest and loyal?**

Names:	Why do you rate them so highly?

The individuals and organizations you listed have the habit of living the Scout Law. As we said earlier in this chapter, most individuals companies that are successful over the long run have made these principles part of who they are. We have seen in the case studies that leaders set the example for other's behavior. Did you and your organization make the list? Why or why not? If not, there are probably some things you can learn from your own responses.

Using Laws to Guide Behavior

Realizing the Scout Law's power in our lives and organizations is possible because of two additional natural laws: the **Law of Expectation** and the **Law of the Garden**. They are self-evident truths that govern our behavior and influence our opportunities for success. The Law of Expectation says: *When we expect something to happen, we tend to act in ways that make it more likely to occur.* The Law of the Garden says: *What we plant, when we plant it and the care we give it determines what we reap.* Both laws are evident in our daily lives and experience.

Think back on a time when you knew you were going to have a disagreement with another person. It might have been with your spouse, partner, parent, boss, teacher, employee, or a best friend. Did you end up with the argument you expected? The answer for most of us is a resounding yes. If you have ever experienced that situation, you understand the Law of Expectation.

Think back on your behavior in that situation. Were you defensive in your communication? Did you accuse the other person of something just so it would hurt or embarrass them? Did you allow your anger and frustration to come through in your conversation? If the answer to any of these questions was yes, then you are beginning to understand how the Law of Expectation works. Our thoughts influence our actions, and when we think we are going to be in a difficult situation, we start responding to our expectations even before the situation arises.

The Law of Expectation works in a positive manner, too. If we expect others to trust us, we act trustworthy. If we expect others to see us as kind and considerate, we act in that manner. By unleashing the power of expectation, we can influence our behavior and, to some degree, the behavior of others.

When focused on the Scout Law, the Law of the Garden builds on the Law of Expectation and helps us to build strong relationships with others. Randy's father planted a small garden for many years—always planted tomatoes. Never once, however, did he go back into the house and say, "I just planted tomatoes out there. I hope we don't get cucumbers coming up." It is a safe bet that if tomatoes are planted, tomatoes will come up...assuming that they are planted at the right time and given the proper care.

We receive the trust and loyalty of others when we plant and cultivate trust and loyalty. We receive kindness and courtesy from others when we invest kindness and courtesy into every interaction. There is, of course, no guarantee that everyone with whom we come into contact will respond consistently with the way we treat them. They are operating within their own expectations. However, there is very little chance of them responding with trust, loyalty, and helpfulness if we do not invest those things into the relationship. The following activities will help you make the Law of Expectation and the Law of the Garden a habit in your individual and organizational life:

- **Decide to make a change.**

All lasting change begins with an internal desire to do something different. For most people, that decision is brought on by a crisis. They find themselves in a difficult situation and have no choice but to do something different. For individuals, the crisis may be the loss of a job, a relationship that has taken a turn for the worse, or a conflict with a boss, employee, or co-worker. For organizations, the crisis may be the loss of a key customer, low morale, or poor quality products and services.

There is another reason to change, however. Successful people and companies have learned to look for opportunities and make changes to take advantage of them. Would your relationships with others be more rewarding if there was a higher degree of trust? Would communication be improved if everyone involved were more friendly, courteous, and kind? Would your organization be more successful if there was a greater sense of loyalty among customers, employees, and suppliers? Would your family, community, and even your business be more successful if everyone obeyed the rules, kept their environment clean, or showed a sense of bravery in addressing the problems that exist? Successful leaders respond to crises as they occur, but most important, they look for opportunities to improve themselves and others.

- **Define what each aspect of the Scout Law means to you.**

What would you and/or your organization be doing differently if the principles described in the Scout Law were being used everyday? What actions could you point out to an uninvolved third party to prove, for instance, you are being trustworthy, loyal, helpful, or friendly? What performance would you want your customers, employees, or suppliers to say demonstrates your bravery, kindness, or obedience? Define the specific behaviors that would indicate to you that each aspect of the Law is being put into practice.

- **Determine what's getting in the way.**

Deciding to make a change puts us on the road to change, but desire alone will not lead to improved performance. Individuals often find that their habits prevent them from making behavioral change. The same is true for organizations. But what creates those habits? The answer is, our behavior repeated over time. Perhaps we need additional knowledge or new skills. Our good intentions are often frustrated by our inability to know what to do and how to do it. Additionally, systems and structures create habits in organizations of all types and sizes. For instance, the system for processing customer complaints may lead people to believe we are not being courteous. Families have ingrained systems for how they divide the tasks to be done within the home. Supervisors and employees have certain routines they go through to communicate, although no written policies exist. Before we can develop new habits, we must first determine what systems, structures, and skills are in place that reinforce the status quo or prevent us from making a change.

- **Develop new habits.**

We are all driven by our habits. We depend on them to help us accomplish routine tasks and free our mind to focus on more important things. But, habits can be harmful also. For instance, the habit of driving on the right side of the road can cause problems when visiting Europe.

Replacing a habit is no easy task. Even with the knowledge of what to do, skills to ensure we know how to do it, and a strong desire to make a change, many people still have difficulty breaking their old habits. The main reason is that we grow comfortable with our old habits, and new behaviors are very uncomfortable until they become habits. Think of the first day in your new exercise program. Were you tired, out of breath, and uncomfortable? Probably. How did you feel the second day? Most people say worse because now they were sore then on top of being tired, out of breath, and uncomfortable. But how did you feel on day number 28? Those who make it that far say, "great"! Everyone else responds with, "I don't know I never made it to 28 days."

The best way to get rid of an old habit is to replace it with a new one. In other words, we must commit ourselves to using our new knowledge and skills consistently with our desire. One must write often to become a great writer; play golf regularly to become a better golfer; and be trustworthy in every encounter to earn the trust of others. Ben Franklin understood the importance of developing good habits. He identified 13 virtues that he believed would help him live a moral life, and created a plan to incorporate them into his behavior by focusing on them one at a time. Each week Franklin would concentrate on one virtue, in essence leaving his performance in the other areas to chance. Each evening he would evaluate his performance and record any shortcomings that occurred. If he went an entire week without a setback, he would move to the next virtue.[10] We can learn a lot about developing new habits from Franklin—break the task down into achievable tasks, pay attention to performance every day, and be totally honest with yourself when evaluating results.

- **Evaluate progress and learn from mistakes.**

Notice that Franklin was never satisfied until he had mastered a concept and completely developed a new habit. For most of us (including Ben Franklin) mastering the habits defined by the Scout Law will take longer than one week. Leaders evaluate their progress as they develop a new habit and then re-evaluate their performance periodically to ensure that they are still on track. Most important, they learn from past mistakes and incorporate that learning into their future performance. Thomas H. Raddal said, "Don't brood on what's past, but don't forget it either." The ability to use less than perfect performance as an opportunity for learning and improvement is a hallmark of leaders who build trust, loyalty, and commitment in themselves and others.

The Scout Law defines principles that, if mastered, earn us the trust, loyalty, respect, friendship, and support of others. In today's changing world, we need strong relationships built on these sound principles to survive and succeed.

"ON MY HONOR, I WILL"

Things I will do to honor my commitment to keep the Scout Law.

NOTES

CHAPTER 7

TO HELP OTHER PEOPLE AT ALL TIMES

Almost anyone will help other people sometimes—people who honor themselves and others help people at all times. They know that our mutual survival and success are connected. In the previous chapter we discussed the importance of laws that yield predictable results. The Law of Reciprocity applies to everything we do. If we help other people at all times, then we are ultimately helped in return. "Giving to get" should not be your primary motivation, but "give and it shall be given to you" is a principle that transcends borders.

Who are these "other people" we should be helping at all times? From a business perspective, there are three groups: customers, employees, and community. Like other principles in this book, the concept of helping others at all times applies in our personal lives as well. Highest on our priority list should be those we *love*, followed by those we *like*, those with and for whom we *work*, those in our *community*, our *country*, and the *world at large*.

Our destinies and our futures are inextricably intertwined, like shipmates on the same ocean liner. Those in the stern cannot refuse to help if they hear water pouring into the bow, even though the bow is far away. The reason is simple: if the bow sinks, the stern follows. As shipmates, we not only share common disaster, but common good. If the bow sails safely into the harbor of success, the stern arrives as well.

It is one thing to decide to help others, but how do we help them? The main thing to remember is that genuine help means giving them what they need—not necessarily what we want them to have. True help means assisting them in obtaining their goals, not enlisting their aid in helping us obtain our own.

What would you think if a pesky neighbor rang your doorbell at 6:00 a.m. one Saturday morning and announced, "I've come over to help you paint your house orange!" You'd probably reply, "I don't want to paint my house, and if I did, I certainly wouldn't paint it orange." Suppose he got angry and shouted, "Your house needs painting, and I got the orange paint on sale! What's the matter with you, don't you want your house to look nice? Boy, some people just don't appreciate someone who tries to help!"

We behave just as foolishly when we try to help others obtain what we want them to have instead of what they want. To be a real help, in the tradition or leadership, we must find what they want and need and assist them in meeting their goals. To build strong relationships grounded in trust, we must, like the Gospel writer Luke, define a leader as one who serves.[1]

How do you find out what people want and need? The answer is surprisingly simple: You ask them.

Peter Megargee Brown, in his book *The Art Of Questioning*,[2] says, "At the start of World War II the story went around that the United States Army spent millions of dollars researching which soldiers should be sent to the warm climates of the South Pacific and which should be sent to the cold northern climates of Europe...army officials finally came to the conclusion...simply to ask the soldiers this question: 'Do you like warm weather or cold weather?' The problem was solved." The same approach works when leaders want to know the needs of their others. They just ask and then listen.

Helping Customers at All Times

Ralph Waldo Emerson observed, "Society is always taken by surprise at any new example of common sense." It's not surprising that successful leaders and organizations help their customers get what they want and need at all times. What is surprising is that more people haven't figured out that helping others succeed is important to their success. Michael LeBoeuf, Ph.D., cites the following statistics that demonstrate the impact of our willingness to help our customers succeed:

- "A typical business hears from only 4 percent of its dissatisfied customers. The other 96 percent go quietly away and 91 percent will never come back."
- In a survey of why customers quit, "68 percent quit because of an attitude of indifference toward the customer by the owner, manager, or some employee."

- "Businesses having low service quality average only a 1 percent return on sales and lose market share at the rate of 2 percent per year. Businesses with high service quality average a 12 percent return on sales, gain market share at the rate of 6 percent a year and charge significantly higher prices."[3]

From a business perspective, it is the customer who pays the bills, finances the growth, and makes it possible to stay in business. Creating and keeping customers is every employee's most important priority. Helping customers at all times then, is the lifeblood of any organization.

What does it mean to help customers at all times? It means working as hard as we can to give them what they want, the way they want it, at the time they want it, and at a price they are willing to pay. Whether your customer is internal or external, your success depends on helping them at all times.

Most people operate this way sometimes. Companies during start-up are hungry for customers and treat each one with dignity and respect. Unfortunately, as the business grows, it becomes more and more difficult to maintain that initial level of customer service. At this point, small organizations sometimes lose some customers because they just don't have the staff or systems to maintain the quality of service their customers expect. In larger organizations, complacency often creeps in as employees decide that much service really isn't necessary and management decides it's okay to lose a few customers, since there are plenty of others who do business with the firm. Large or small, any business who decides customers are expendable is doomed.

Marc was arranging a large party at a restaurant, the owner attempted to change both the agreed upon price and the menu—claiming his wife had agreed to it. (She had not.) When he was unsuccessful at obtaining the original menu, he reluctantly said he would have to have to cancel because his wife would never be happy with the menu as it was now presented. Marc realized any possibility of successful negotiation was over when the owner said, "I'm not in business just to satisfy people and make people happy; I'm in business to make money!" Marc's response was, "any organization that's not in business to satisfy customers and make them happy cannot possibly stay in business!" The restaurant closed less than six months later.

Here are a few points to remember as you work to help satisfy your customers and make them happy!

- **Perception is reality**. If the customer says you aren't meeting their needs, then you aren't meeting their needs. Period.
- **Little things mean a lot**. You demonstrate your commitment to helping the customer through the little things that you do. Paying attention to the details sends a message of integrity and concern. As one executive says, "Take care of the little things, and the big things often take care of themselves."
- **Complaints are good news.** This sounds strange, but people and organizations learn from customer feedback. If someone takes the time to let us know how they feel, it is important that

we listen to their opinion. Ken Blanchard, Ph.D., and Spencer Johnson, M.D., writing in *The One Minute Manager,*[4] make the statement, "Feedback is the breakfast of champions." Good organizations want to hear what their customers have to say.

- **Great service doesn't take the place of quality products; you must have both.** There are people and organizations who assume that a smile and an apology will make up for lack of quality...it won't. A smile and an apology will work once, but the quality must be there if you want them to keep coming back.

- **There are two components to quality products and services.** The first component is *doing it right the first time*. The second is *having systems in place to catch and correct mistakes* when they do occur.

- **Everyone likes to feel good about themselves**. People want to feel they made the right decision, that they are important, and that they are valuable. People like to do business and associate with people who make them feel important.

Employees must carry the message that the organization wants to help customers at all times. Leaders and organizations of integrity understand the relationship between helping employees and helping customers, and they actively work to make the employee/customer connection a positive one. J.W. (Bill) Marriott, Chairman and President of the Marriott Corporation, emphasizes the employee connection with these words, "Motivate them, train them, care about them, and make winners out of them…we know that if we treat our employees correctly, they'll treat the customers right. And if customers are treated right, they'll come back."[5] Since taking care of your employees is so important to taking care of your customers, let's take a look at how you can help them!

Helping Employees at All Times

Ask a typical executive what their employees want from a job and the response will be, "Money." If he or she has a moment to think about it, he often adds "security." Money and security are important, but they aren't all today's worker wants from a job. The most important thing a worker wants is job satisfaction. Job satisfaction includes pay and security, as well as opportunity, fulfillment, encouragement, coaching, a sense of partnership, and respect. Helping them means providing skills, support, opportunity, and role models to assist them in obtaining satisfaction in their jobs. When it comes to pay, we believe employees also want their compensation to be based on the work they do and the importance of that work—not just by job title or classification.

Management consultant Steve Ventura uses the following exercise to drive home the importance of money for job satisfaction:

- **Think of your favorite job of all time, the one you would choose if you could have any job you wanted. Write that job in the space provided.**

- **Would you do that job for:**

1 percent less that you make today?	___ Yes	___ No
5 percent less that you make today?	___ Yes	___ No
10 percent less that you make today?	___ Yes	___ No
25 percent less that you make today?	___ Yes	___ No

Most people respond that they would do their "favorite" job for 1 percent less than they make today. Few say yes to a 25 percent decrease. Somewhere between 1 percent and 25 percent, our life style, obligations, financial goals, and values take over and influence the response. The point is, that if you answered yes to doing a job for 1 percent less than you make today, you have said other things are as or more important to you than money.

- **In the space provided, list the job factors that you consider part of your "ideal job."**

If you found these factors to be important in your ideal job, do you think others will too? So do we!

Ask children what they want to be when they grow up and watch them play make-believe. They'll tell you they want to be doctors, cowboys, cowgirls, ball players, pilots, firefighters, etc. The common factor is that the vocations they aspire to are those that will make them feel important. No one ever pretends to be someone who is bored, angry, and unappreciated.

Children get excited about their "ideal jobs." Adults do too! There are many employees in every organization hoping for that "ideal job." Participative management, quality circles, and self-managed work teams are all great tools to help give employees what they want. Unfortunately, many of these programs achieve less than satisfactory results. Judith Vogt and Bradley Hunt, writing in the May 1988, *Training and Development Journal* suggest that 50 percent of current participative work groups will dissolve. We believe that the root cause of the failure is a lack of trust—which is another way of saying that they doubt the integrity of management. Before you can help employees create their ideal job, they have to trust your motives and intentions.

How to Know if There Is a Perceived Lack of Integrity

There are many excellent tools available to determine employee perceptions. Whether your organization is large or small, here are some simple ways to "check the pulse." You'll know there's lack of trust when you find:

- **Decreased support for the organization's mission and vision**

- **Increased turnover**
- **Increased absenteeism not related to specific illness**
- **Increased number of disputes, complaints, or grievances**
- **Questioning of management support for new initiatives or changes**
- **Increased reliance on outside or formal sources to resolve issues of "unfair treatment."**

When employees repeatedly question your motives or intentions, it's usually because they got burned in the past. Maybe not by you, but burned nevertheless. We all carry the baggage of experience into each new situation. If that experience was bad, our baggage is often filled with mistrust.

How to Get Integrity Back on Track

The fact you want to build or regain credibility and are committed to leading with integrity is a good start to getting integrity in your workplace back on track. The people you lead will soon know whether or not you're sincere. Your commitment will be proven, over time, by your actions. Here are some ideas to get integrity back on track where you work:

- **Ask employees for their perceptions.** If they don't trust you, they may not be honest with you, so provide a way for them to give you anonymous feedback.

- **Acknowledge their perceptions.** Feelings are neither right nor wrong—they're just feelings. You may disagree with what they say, but don't be defensive. You are all working toward a common goal—a better relationship.

- **Acknowledge your shortcomings.** Admit it when you have acted inappropriately. We all have a great capacity for forgiveness when someone confesses a fault freely.

- **Realize the process takes time.** Problems take time to develop, solutions take time to implement, perceptions take time to change.

- **Continually ask for feedback.** Periodically, ask people how you're doing and listen to their comments. Your willingness to ask and listen sends a message that you understand the importance of credibility, trust, and integrity.

- **Treat people with dignity and respect at all times.** Educator Booker T. Washington, writer of the classic book *Up From Slavery* and founder of the Tuskegee Institute, said, "There can be no real social progress in this country until we realize there is as much dignity in tilling a field as there is in writing a poem." Not as much *money*—as much *dignity*. The janitor is not entitled to as much money as the president, but he or she deserves as much dignity.

A comedian once lamented, "No good deed goes unpunished." Sometimes, even when we do the right thing for the right reasons, it doesn't turn out as we might have wished. A leader may invest a lot of time and talent in helping and developing a subordinate, then the subordinate will leave. This should not discourage us. People who are going to leave are going to leave regardless. Your efforts to help that person be all he or she can be means their association with you was more valuable while they were there. Your personal interest may have enabled them to find opportunities in your organization longer and thus have prolonged their stay. (Besides, there is something worse than spending the time and money to train a person and having them leave, and that is not training them and having them stay!)

LEADERSHIP IN ACTION: MARY KAY ASH

Mary Kay Ash founded Mary Kay Cosmetics in 1963, and since that time, it has grown to more than 200,000 employees and beauty consultants in twelve countries, with wholesale sales of more than $450 million a year! How did it begin? Mary Kay says,

> **"I had opinions about the organizations I'd worked for. There had been many things I thought should have been done another way...I decided to write my memoirs—actually, a book that would help other women overcome some of the obstacles I had encountered. First, I wrote down all the good things the companies I had been with had done and then the changes I would make to create a company that was based on the Golden Rule. Wouldn't it be marvelous, I kept thinking, if someone would actually start such a company? And then I realized that I didn't have to sit and wish—I could start that dream company because I had already**

> discovered the ideal product…To me, "P" and
> "L" meant more than *profit* and *loss*—it meant
> *people* and *love.*" [6]

People and love are descriptive words for Mary Kay Cosmetics. Mary Kay Ash doesn't just talk about loving people—she lives it. That's what has made her one of the most respected businesspeople in America. The love begins with her sales force and employees, and it extends to customers.

Mary Kay Ash believes that you must lead with integrity, whether you're leading an organization, a work unit, or oneself. Integrity means you put God first, family second, and career third. She believes leaders must "walk their talk" in order to get the message across. While the company doesn't force religion on anyone, Mary Kay says that by setting the example, people come to their own conclusion that her philosophy is for real.

Not many companies would blatantly say that they want you to place your family above your career. Those that do are often strapped for positive examples of how they put that into action—not so at Mary Kay Cosmetics. The proof is in the performance. Company employees are told anytime there's a family need, all they have to do to be excused from work is notify their manager. Family is so important to the company that each year they invite employees and their families to the Six Flags Over Texas amusement park for their company picnic—and pick up all the expenses. They give turkeys to all employees the Monday before Thanksgiving (so the birds have time to properly thaw) and share the cost of annual mammograms for female employees.

In addition to promoting strong family values, they also try to maintain a family atmosphere at work. It's an informal company, and there are no titles on any of the office doors.

Everyone knows that top sales people at Mary Kay get a pink Cadillac. But the company does a great job of training and encouraging at all levels to get them to that Cadillac. No matter how many mistakes are made, they focus the trainee on what went right—not what went wrong. Each consultant receives a ribbon for her first $100 show, another for her first $200 show, and so on. Milestones are marked with diamond rings, and trips abroad. At awards ceremonies, as many people as possible are publicly rewarded and praised. They honor initial and entry level achievements all the way up to the crowning of the queens, complete with a satin sashes, tiaras, a bouquet of long-stemmed roses (pink, of course), and prizes like diamond rings, mink coats—and the crown jewels— diamond bumble bees! Why bumble bees? Because it is aerodynamically impossible for the bumble bee to fly, because of its weight and wing configuration—but the bumble bee doesn't know it and flies anyway!

With this much enthusiasm, some are initially skeptical. Many people find it hard to believe that Mary Kay Cosmetics is for real, but it is. In a world filled with hyperbole and sales hype, it's easy to become somewhat jaundiced about a company's claims to care. Executives at Mary Kay know that, and they are patient, believing that integrity will eventually win the skeptical over. Mary Kay Ash herself puts it simply, "When you walk your talk, people know it and respond positively."

Mary Kay considers customers part of the family too. The company offers a money-back guarantee on all merchandise sold—even if the container is empty when it's returned. They have a staff of medically-trained professionals and a laboratory to answer questions about any adverse reactions to a product.

Mary Kay Ash leads with integrity for two reasons:

- she knows that's the way she wants to be treated
- she knows that helping employees, sales people, and customers at all times is good business

Satisfying the needs of others is what leading with integrity is all about. Take care of others and they will take care of you.

LEADERSHIP IN ACTION: SEWELL LEXUS

Carl Sewell's automobile dealerships not only sell Lexus, but Cadillac, Oldsmobile, and Hyundai cars. He has built his company into one of the top car dealerships in America. He didn't start that way, but he reached his goal by continually applying one simple principle—turning "one time" buyers into lifetime customers.

How does Sewell build customers for life? For the details, we recommend that you read his book, but in general, he continually helps employees and customers. Examples abound:

- free loan cars
- extended service hours (Saturdays and evenings)
- personal contact with customers
- attention to detail (grounds, cars, restrooms)

- incentives and rewards for employees that help turn prospects into customers for life

Sewell's philosophy and systems set the standard, but it is the performance of individuals who really make the difference. At Sewell, there are leaders at every turn, and their willingness to help others is a primary reason for everyone's individual and collective success.

Rob Schweizer is not the stereo typical car salesperson. You notice it right away by the questions he asks, and, most important, by the way he listens. It is common for an automobile sales professional to establish contact with a potential customer by asking something such as "May I help you?" It is uncommon for them to listen for your response. The behavior that has given car sales professional something of a bad name goes something like this:

> Salesperson: " May I help you?"
> Customer: "No thanks, I'm just looking"
> Salesperson: "How much were you thinking about spending on a car?"

It is obvious where this conversation is going. In contrast, Rob asks a different question. You can expect something such as "Do you have something special in mind?" or "Can I answer any questions for you?"

It's a little thing, but it sets the tone for a positive relationship. Asking about price is perceived as a qualifying technique to determine if the customer is worth pursing. Asking "how I can help" initiates a relationship built on honesty, open communication, and mutual success.

Rob's example continues in other ways. While one couple discussed how good a specific car would look with tinted windows, he was listening for an opportunity to help, instead of looking for an add-on feature to sell. Rob presented the car, with windows tinted, when the customers came to pick it up. There was, of course, no additional charge.

Cecily McClarin is another leader who helps others succeed. She demonstrates her commitment from the rather unlikely position of the finance department. Every financial professional is at least courteous to customers. After all, they want you to purchase the automobile. Few, however, become part of the service team.

Cecily, like Rob, focuses on little things such as volunteering to check for alternative financing to reduce monthly payments and intervening one year after the sale to correct problems related to the automobile registration.

Does helping others help Rob and Cecily on a personal level. For Rob, the answer is obviously yes. Satisfied customers breed repeat business. For Cecily, the answer is less obvious, but one could make a case that she benefits through continued employment. Yet, experience tells us that prospects of repeat business and even continued employment are not, in and of themselves, enough to motivate people to help others at all times. If that were true, the perception of car dealers as less than honorable would not exist. Rob and Cecily see themselves as leaders, not of people, but as professionals. They take personal responsibility for the success of others, and in doing so, influence their own long-term success.

In *Customers for Life,*[7] Sewell gives his views on integrity. "People spend an awful lot of time watching what the boss does. And if the boss wants his employees to act ethically, he'd better behave that way himself...We tell our people they should always ask themselves, 'How would my actions appear if they were described tomorrow on the front page of the local newspaper?' "

It's obvious that Carl Sewell believes his words. It is also obvious that his employees and customers do too!

Helping Communities at All Times

Helping people takes getting involved. It is caring, and sharing, and service in action. A whole nation was ashamed when a woman was raped in broad daylight on a public sidewalk and other pedestrians merely stopped to watch. We are not a nation of cowards, but even if everyone in the crowd lacked the physical or moral courage to come to the woman's aid, couldn't someone have at least summoned aid? If we reap what we sow, what happens when we ignore crime in the streets, hopelessness, illiteracy, environmental hazards, or political corruption because we don't want to "get involved"? Unfortunately, we are sensing the impact of our apathy playing itself out in communities throughout our nation.

Martin Neimoller, a Lutheran pastor in Nazi Germany in the 1930s, summed up eloquently the final result of failure to be involved: "In Germany, they came first for the communists, and I didn't speak up because I wasn't a communist. Then they came for the Jews, and I didn't speak up because I wasn't a Jew. Then they came for the trade unionists, and I didn't speak up because I wasn't a trade unionist. Then they came for the Catholics, and I didn't speak up because I was a Protestant. Then they came for me, and by that time, no one was left to speak up." Neimoller lived to know the full import of the words Edmund Burke wrote 150 years earlier, "The only thing necessary for the triumph of evil is for enough good men to do nothing."

Leaders feel that helping others "is their job"—and they teach others to feel the same way. When Robert Haas took over Levi Strauss and Company in 1984, he called his executives together and told them he would require them to disclose how they had contributed to the success of others at salary and performance reviews. Haas wanted to know what each executive had done to ensure the company's success, but he felt their contributions to the success of others within the organization and the community was just as important. Today, leaders everywhere are encouraging contribution to the community. And they are providing positive role models for those they lead. No one, for instance, forces leaders such as David Kearns, retired CEO at Xerox, to head up One-To-One, a partnership between business and volunteer organizations that provides mentoring to "at risk" youth. Likewise, Harold S. Hook, Chairman and CEO of American General Corporation volunteers in positions from local Troop Leader to President of the Boy Scouts National Board because he believes in helping others succeed and knows that he benefits when the community benefits.

Helping our communities requires that we help them determine what they need in addition to listening to what they want. As Booker T. Washington said, "If you give a man a fish, you give him a meal. If you teach him how to fish, he can feed himself—and someone else too." True help is encouraging and empowering another to be all they can be. After all, a best friend is someone who brings out the best in you, and not merely someone who tells you things are fine when they aren't. A friend tells you what's wrong and helps you make it right. A friend encourages you to do your best to fix the problem. Leaders serve their community in ways that not only meet immediate needs, but foster solutions.

If everyone looked to help others at all times, there would be no problem hazardous waste, no abandoned neighborhoods, no problems with gangs, and no literacy problems. There would be no homeless problem, and very little need for a welfare system. There would have been no need for President Bush's "thousand points of light" speech—or for this book. Helping our communities is "love your neighbor as yourself" in action.

LEADERSHIP IN ACTION: DR. STANLEY PEARLE

Dr. Stanley Pearle founded Pearl Vision in 1961 with the opening of the first store in Savannah, Georgia. Today, Pearle, Inc. is part of Grand Metropolitan and is the largest retail optical company in the world—with over one thousand stores in the United States, Puerto Rico, Canada, Taiwan, Japan, the Netherlands, and Belgium. Dr. Pearl serves as a consultant to the company and participates in meetings of the Pearle Executive Committee. He says, "We began with the philosophy that the public would respond favorably to conveniently located, attractive optical centers that offered a combination of quality products, a large selections of styles, reasonable prices, and most importantly, a staff of competent personnel who could provide excellent professional services." Dr. Pearle is fond of saying, "The customer is smarter than you think. You must deliver what you promise. That is the only way to develop trust."

Dr. Pearle has worked to extend the concept of integrity throughout the organization. His leadership style emphasizes fair compensation, promotions based on merit, responsibility, candidness, and truthfulness. Most promotions are made from within the company. Dr. Pearle often cites the example of Del McNally, who began as a stock clerk in 1966 and rose to become a vice president of merchandising and the largest purchaser of eyewear frames in the world.

Dr. Pearle believes that management has an obligation to give something back to the community in addition to helping the company grow. He has been active in community affairs and served as president of both the Dallas United Way and the Jewish Foundation. He gives a lot of credit in the building of his character to his experiences first as a Boy Scout and later as an Assistant Scout Master.

About community service he says, "You shouldn't brag about your community service or people will doubt your integrity. Also, you shouldn't do community service for business gain, but simply because it's the right thing to do."

Howard Stanworth, former President and CEO of Pearle, Inc., agrees. He says, "All citizens, individual or corporate, have a responsibility for the social health of the community, as well as their own financial well-being. Commerce should provide constructive community support from the inside and understand the issues which preserve good quality of life for the members of that community, whether those issues relate to the environment, employment, security, or education."

In 1987, the company created the Pearle Vision Foundation dedicated to the preservation and optimization of lifetime vision. It delivers direct benefits to hardship cases requiring urgent care. The foundation has provided treatment for cataracts, eye muscle disorders, and sight-threatening accidents, as well as eye exams and eyeglasses for disadvantaged families.

Grand Metropolitan, Pearle Inc.'s parent company, also has a long tradition of community involvement. Sir Allen Sheppard, Chairman of the Board, clearly stated the organization's position in the following statement:

"At Grand Metropolitan, we measure performance by profitability and return on investment, but there is another significant measure—how we fulfill our responsibility to the communities from which our profits are derived...It is not just sound business sense for us to care about the environment and communities within which we work and live, it is common sense to contribute to the quality of life in our communities."

The corporate philosophy at Grand Metropolitan is summed up in a simple phrase: "We aim to help people in need help themselves."

There is an old parable about a visitor who was shown two banquet halls filled with people. In the first hall, no one was eating. When the visitor asked why, he was told that the king had tied a long spoon to each guest's arms and they couldn't bend their elbows. Therefore, although the table was loaded with food, no one was able to convey it to their mouth! In the next room, everyone was eating and having a wonderful time. Oh, these guests also had the long spoons tied to their arms—but each guest fed someone else! By helping others, we help ourselves.

While serving in the White House, President Ronald Reagan had a sign on his desk that read, "There is no limit to what you can accomplish if you don't care who gets the credit." Likewise, there is no limit to what we can accomplish in helping others if we don't care who gets the credit. The examples listed here have primarily focused on the involvement of well known business and civic leaders. Yet, we know that there are thousands of "unknown leaders" giving their time, energy, and resources to help others at work and in their communities. They do not invest themselves for personal gain, although they may be recognized for their efforts. Their motivation comes from a sense of commitment and knowledge that by helping others they ultimately help themselves.

Following is a questionnaire to help you evaluate what kind of job you're currently doing to help other people at all times. Afterwards, there's a commitment sheet to help you focus on how you can do more.

Helping Other People Questionnaire

- In what activities are you currently involved for the purpose of helping other people?

  _____

  _____

  _____

  _____

- What is the scope of your involvement? (Time, money, organizational resources, etc.)

  _____

  _____

  _____

  _____

- What do you expect in return for your involvement in these activities?

  _____

  _____

  _____

  _____

- What have you received from your involvement in these activities?

  _____

  _____

  _____

  _____

- What impact has your involvement had on the success of others?

  _____

  _____

  _____

  _____

In an earlier chapter, we quoted John Donne's admonition to remember that all of mankind is tied together in life and death. We are not only diminished by death, but by inefficiency, insecurity, lack of knowledge, lack of resources, and lack of opportunities. The Boy Scouts knew, in 1907, that helping others is a mandate for success, character, and our mutual survival in changing times. Generations before and since have realized the same thing. We hope you will realize it, too...and act on it daily.

"ON MY HONOR, I WILL"

Things I will do to help other people at all times.

```
NOTES
```

CHAPTER 8

TO KEEP MYSELF PHYSICALLY STRONG, MENTALLY AWAKE, AND MORALLY STRAIGHT

Survival and success in a challenging, and often hostile, world depends on our ability to effectively respond to any situation. The pledge to keep oneself physically strong, mentally awake, and morally straight recognizes the role of body, mind, and spirit in creating a healthy individual, prepared to meet the challenges and opportunities that arise. Although the world has changed since Scouting's inception, the importance of being personally prepared to survive and succeed in an often hostile world has not diminished.

Thanks to the work of dedicated healthcare professionals such as Bernie Siegel, M.D.,[1] and Carl and Stephanie Simonton, many have learned specific techniques to control their own health. The Simontons and James L. Creighton state in their book *Getting Well Again*,[2] "Everyone participates in his or her health or illness at all times." The foundations of holistic medicine stand on the three-legged stool of body, mind, and spirit. We can be prepared to met the challenges of a changing world by mastering all three.

A promise to remain physically strong, mentally awake, and morally straight uses the same components to ensure preparation for success in honoring commitments and providing leadership. Being physically strong and mentally awake prepares the leader to meet and deal with challenges as they arise. Being morally straight guides our actions by ensuring their consistency with accepted values. All three work together to ensure success.

To Keep Myself Physically Strong

Today, few Americans earn their living through sheer physical strength. Most of the strenuous physical labor once done by men and women is done by machines, or are machine-assisted. This has not changed the necessity to remain physically strong. In fact, the increased use of machines means we must take even more responsibility for our own health and vitality. The Simontons and James Creighton report that the rise in heart disease and cancer parallels the rise of affluent, sedentary life styles that accompanied increased industrialization. One reason for the decrease in our physical strength is that we are eating more and eating the wrong things while doing less—a situation easily remedied.

A second reason for the decreased state of our health is increased stress. People often laugh when a friend longs for the simpler life of the "good old days." But it's true that life was simpler a couple of generations back. Today, we live in a stressful world, and stress not only affects us mentally, it affects us physically as well. As long ago as the 1920s, Hans Selye at the University of Prague found a strong connection between stress and physical strength. He noted that stress can affect bodily functions, cause hormonal imbalances, lead to damaged arteries, and result in immune system malfunctions.

Our early ancestors had a way of dealing with stress: Immediately following a stressful situation, they reacted physically by fight or flight. This was true whether the stress came from a mastodon attack or an arrow in the shoulder. Many of the situations in which we find ourselves today do not offer the opportunity for physical release. Without that release, the body builds up stress, affecting our ability to perform at our best, and possibly causing physical problems as well. If stress is a part of your life, there are several good books on the subject that can either help eliminate the stress or help control your reaction to it.

Becoming physically strong is primarily a matter of becoming physically fit. Physical fitness, according to George Sheehan, III, M.D., makes a person feel at home in their environment and better enables him to make responses or perform acts. It also counterbalances the results of a sedentary life style.

There are a number of good books and programs available for becoming physically fit. We suggest you consult your physician about your individual needs. If you haven't engaged in physical activity for a while, doing too much too soon can be dangerous. As a rule of thumb, however, we like the principles of fitness Sheehan provided in an essay entitles "Fitness Enhances the Quality of Your Life." [3] They are:

- eat a good breakfast
- don't eat between meals
- maintain your weight
- don't smoke
- exercise regularly and sensibly

Sheehan suggests that the benefits of exercise are both physiological and psychological. In other words, it helps you reverse the effects of an inactive life style and helps you deal with the stress of life. We agree. There's nothing like exercise to release the tension, even if it is something as unglamorous as cleaning the attic.

In addition to these tips, we recommend that you investigate and implement other activities to manage your stress and balance your life. Marjorie Blanchard, Ph.D., has developed a model for maintaining a balanced life. The model, described by the acronym PACT, outlines four areas that affect a feeling of balance and reduce stress. She encourages people to work on the following areas in her essay entitled "Make a PACT to Balance Your Life"[4]:

- **Perspective** - The ability to take a "big picture" view of the events surrounding you.
- **Autonomy** - The feeling of individual control of events and outcomes.
- **Connectedness** - The quality of your relationships and a feeling of contentment with your physical environment.
- **Tone** - How you feel about yourself physically.

Today's leaders must have physical stamina to compete in a global market place. The increased stamina will result in increased productivity, a more energetic leadership style, less stress, and longer life.

A lady of Marc's acquaintance bought a home in a small, rural Texas town when she turned 60, thinking she would live out her last few years in the town where she grew up. Now 100 years of age, she is still there, living alone, and in excellent health. (In fact, she still does all her own yard work.) Marc asked her, "Are you glad you moved here 39 years ago?" She immediately snapped, "No! If I'd known I was going to live this long, I'd have moved somewhere more exciting where I didn't have to work so hard!" Little did she know a low-stress rural environment and undertaking all her own yard work probably contributed to these added years.

Mentally Awake

Baden-Powell drew on his experience as an Army Scout when creating the Boy Scout program. He knew that a scout must be mentally awake or the enemy might slip through the line of defense, or he might miss some vital information.

Although the physical dangers facing us today are not the same, they do exist. With the rise in crime and terrorism, we must always be "mentally awake" as we go about our lives. Today's leaders must also be mentally awake to what's going on in their organizations, the marketplace, and the world if they are to compete and lead effectively. In today's world that means being mentally awake to change. To be effective, leaders must be mentally awake to:

- **changing needs of the organization as a whole, whether it is a business, a club, or a family**
- **changing needs of individuals within the organization**
- **changing needs of customers and those who depend on us**
- **changing needs of suppliers or providers**
- **changing needs of the communities in which they live**
- **changes in technology**
- **changes in the actions and behavior of their competitors**

In a world that is exploding with change, the seven last words of any organization are, "We've never done it that way before." Tradition is a fine heritage, but a lousy excuse for missing an opportunity to improve.

Staying mentally awake to opportunities and challenges requires us to look at and seek new information. That means we must be open to change. Most people are in favor of change as long as it doesn't affect them. In our work with organizations and their leaders, we hear many people saying that a change is needed. Most, however, believe that the change should begin with someone else. The typical response is "I am doing things the right way now!" or "I am open to new possibilities; it's the other people who refuse to change." The truth is, change is usually difficult for anyone. Even positive change brings on anxious feelings. But, the alternative to change and adaptation is death. In other words, we must be mentally awake to growth and development; otherwise we will stagnate and perish. Effective leaders accept continuous learning and change as the only way to grow and flourish. They stay mentally awake to embrace change that results in improvement as individuals and organizations.

One way to stay mentally awake to opportunities is to read. Effective leaders read newspapers, journals, magazines, newsletters, books, and anything they can get their hands on to gather information. We know many leaders who regularly read four newspapers every day, and several who read as many as seven. To accomplish this task, they read only those sections that provide them with information they can use. Individuals who believe they don't have time to read the books necessary to stay current in their field might consider subscribing to book summaries, listening to audio cassettes, or taking advantage of the various on-line computer services that are available. It's important to remember that staying mentally awake is more than staying up with the latest business developments. The effective leader also spends time on personal development. He or she knows that self-improvement increases personal willingness and ability to change.

Ed Foreman was a millionaire by the age of 26 and is the only person in the twentieth century to be elected to Congress from two states (Texas and New Mexico). Today, he helps individuals grow and develop through a three day program called "The Successful Life Course." Ed believes that individuals should feed their minds properly if they hope to prepare themselves for success. He recommends:

- **daily reading of inspirational books**
- **listening regularly to positive messages**
- **associating with positive people**
- **thinking about what you want to have happen**

Another way to monitor the need for change is to listen. In organizations, we should listen to customers, employees, peers, suppliers, and even competitors. As individuals, leaders listen to family, friends, and other leaders (even those with views that differ from their own). Most important, they listen to themselves. They monitor their own "inner voice" to determine the need for change and chart a course of action.

Listening is the most used form of communication, and the communication skill least developed. All of us hear, but few really listen. Listening requires us to focus on the message given by the other person or group rather than on the message we want to give. Often, we spend the time when others are speaking to think about what we want to say next, rather than using the opportunity to listen. Corrie Ten Boom, author of the best-selling book *The Hiding Place*,[5] related an instance from her childhood in which she was introduced to an elderly woman. A moment later, Corrie confessed, "I'm sorry, but I've forgotten your name." The elderly woman smiled and said, "That's all right, dear. When someone is introduced the only name they ever hear is their own."

The first goal of communication is to listen and understand. Only when we have done this have we earned the right to be heard and listened to. Effective leadership involves constant two-way communication. The leader uses information gleaned from others to look for new opportunities, stay alert for challenges that might affect success, and keep the organization on track. The leader then uses the information to communicate direction. Stephen Covey, Ph.D., provides a wonderful illustration of the difference between leadership and management in his book

The Seven Habits of Highly Effective People.[6] Covey asks his readers to imagine a group of producers moving through the jungle. The producers are the people doing the work, clearing the jungle with machetes. There are also people responsible for managing the people doing the work. These managers make sure that the work is done properly. They write the procedures and develop the programs to see that the producers are both effective and efficient. There is also a leader on this journey. The leader is the person who climbs a tree now and then to look out over the jungle and make sure the group is in the right jungle. The leader must be mentally awake to recognize the need for change and listen to the information received if the organization is to arrive at its destination.

Morally Straight

Being morally straight keeps the leader moving in a direction that is consistent with the natural laws that contribute to long-term success. Natural laws, as we saw in Chapter 6, are self-evident truths that govern successful relationships and performance. Society's values often ebb and flow according to popular thought. The morally straight leader uses timeless truths to maintain a moral compass that serves as a guide in uncharted territories. Most important, morally straight leaders rarely talk about morality (remember the Emerson quote in Chapter 2 about the spoons?), choosing to live out their moral code and demonstrate their beliefs by action. The moral leader deals with people quietly, on an individual basis, rather than publicly, realizing not everyone has grown to the same state of moral awareness.

It is our belief that the successful leader of the future must, above all else, be morally straight. Society has come to demand that of its leaders in all walks of life. Public officials and personalities displaying poor judgment is not new, but public awareness has increased. Industrial accidents occurred before there were oil spills that damaged the environment; and shady business deals were being done before the savings & loan crisis of the 1980s. In many ways the media, with its ability to draw attention to individual incidents on the other side of the world and bring them to our living rooms in living color, has created an environment where being morally straight is vital to a leader's survival. On the other hand, the public has a tendency to be forgiving and have a short memory when the guilty party readily confesses to the transgression. Three confessions can help any leader get back on track when the moral compass strays off course:

- **I did it.**
- **I'm sorry.**
- **How can I make it right?**

Leadership in a Changing World

The world has changed since the writing of the Boy Scout Oath. There are fewer rivers to be explored and fewer lands to be developed. But today, as then, we need leaders who are physically strong, mentally awake, and morally straight. In fact, we need them more today than ever before. Our world has become more complex despite all the technological advances that have made it more convenient. Change is the order of the day. And its increasing speed technological advances that have made it more convenient. Change is the order of the day. And its increasing speed often prevents us from having the time to think through our responses. Success and survival depend on being capable of meeting the challenge of change through being able to respond to any situation.

"ON MY HONOR, I WILL"

In the space provided, list the actions you will take to honor your commitment to become physically strong, mentally awake, and morally straight.

```
NOTES




```

CHAPTER 9
LIVING THE OATH—LIFE STYLE INTEGRITY

The principles contained in the Scout Oath and Law have provided direction to more than 270 million boys. Since we learn our core values at an early age, it is safe to assume that most of those who received Scout training continue to practice the principles of integrity they learned in Scouting. Add to the 270 million Boy Scouts all those who were Girl Scouts, graduates of religious training programs, or raised by parents who valued honesty, ethics, and integrity; and you have a solid base on which to build a business, a community, a country, and a world. Most of us grew up knowing the difference from right and wrong and the importance of integrity. Most of us consciously avoid violating our values in the important areas of our lives; we don't commit murder, robbery, rape, treason, or any of the "major sins."

The moral crises most of us face are not major, but what some would consider "minor." Yet any deviation from the basic tenets of honor and integrity has potentially catastrophic consequences. As the writer of the Song of

Solomon said, it's the "little foxes that spoil the vines,"[1] and even small leaks, left unchecked, can sink great ships. A slight overcharge on a customer's bill, a small lie to a co-worker, a broken promise, failure to report it when we are undercharged for an item, a missed opportunity to help build our community. These may be little things in the grand scheme of life, but they are corrosive to our ability to built trust and create a society committed to honor and integrity.

The leaders we have profiled know the value of maintaining integrity at all levels and at all times. They echo this statement from John Antioco, CEO at Circle K convenience stores:

"No business or business person can be successful long term without integrity or concern for people. Trust by employees and customers is essential for success. People respect the truth whether it is bad news or good news. Once a company loses the confidence of its employees or customers, it is the beginning of the end. A company exists to serve its customers and reward its employees and stockholders—profits merely allow the company to continue to exist."

Since the truths Antioco spoke of are self-evident, why do we continue to have problems in America? Why is there a lack of trust of leaders in politics, business, and even religion? Is it the short-term focus forced on business today by restless stockholders? Is it a result of increased competitiveness? Is it because employers are treating employees as second-class citizens while asking them to provide first-class treatment to customers? Is it that we are conditioned for immediate gratification and are willing to do whatever it takes to get what we want now? All of these excuses have been given by those who diminish the standards of integrity. Yet, "good excuses" never compensate for good behavior, and we are judged by what we do—not by what we say.

Whatever excuses others find for lack of integrity, you, as a leader with integrity, must walk as you talk. More than that, you must teach others to do the same by creating an environment of integrity and trust in your workplace. Nobody has promised that it will be easy—nothing worthwhile ever is. Building integrity in your workplace takes time, patience, persistence and—most of all—commitment.

JCPenney, is one company with a long history of operating with integrity. We mentioned them briefly in Chapter 1, but let's take a closer look at how they began and how they literally became, "a company built on integrity."

LEADERSHIP IN ACTION: JCPENNEY COMPANY, INC.

On April 14, 1902, 26-year-old James Cash Penney, Thomas M. Callahan, and William Guy Johnson opened the first "Golden Rule Store" in Kemmerer, Wyoming. Over the next several years, as the store prospered, they set up other Golden Rule Stores. Each was operated as a partnership that enabled those responsible for the store's success to share in the profits.

In 1913, when the Golden Rule Stores were incorporated as the JCPenney Company, James Penney met with all the partners in "The Golden Rule" to discuss the new company. He wanted to make certain their new organization had the same motivation, spirit, and ethical foundation that had made the company successful. The 36 men at that meeting adopted a company motto built on four words: Honor, Confidence, Service, Cooperation. This motto was later abbreviated to H.C.S.C. (Honor, Confidence, Service, Cooperation) and used it in the company emblem. That meeting also produced the "Penney Idea," seven principles that guide the company to this day. They are:

1. To serve the public, as nearly as we can, to its complete satisfaction.
2. To expect for the service we render a fair remuneration and not all the profit the traffic will bear.
3. To do all in our power to pack the customer's dollar full of value, quality, and satisfaction.
4. To continue to train ourselves and our associates so that the service we give will be more and more intelligently performed.
5. To improve constantly the human factor in our business.
6. To reward men and women in our organization through participation in what the business produces.
7. To test our every policy, method, and act in this wise: "Does it square with what is right and just?"

Since the beginning, the JCPenney Company has operated on what retired President and CEO, Earl Corder Sames, calls "a certain service we owe to our community...which is merchandise at a fair profit." The result was that JCPenney has become an institution in America. The company has never suffered a serious ethical crisis in its history. W.R. Howell, current Chairman of the Board, shared this example of the integrity of the leaders' who built the company in an October 1990 speech:

"Mr. Penney was on the Board of Directors of a bank in Florida during the Great Depression. He had nothing to do with the day-to-day running of the business, but his name and reputation were instrumental in bringing in depositors. Well, like so many other financial institutions at the time, the bank folded and there was an outcry from depositors. Many could not understand how a bank associated with Mr. Penney could fail while he remained a multi-millionaire. Mr. Penney was so anguished by the event that he used a large part of his personal fortune to pay the depositors what they had lost. He clearly was under no legal obligation to do so. He simply felt it was the right thing to do. That's the kind of person he was— and that's the kind of legacy he left. He never forgot that when you're a company that serves the public, what you are and how you conduct yourself become a part of your name and reputation."

The policies and principles of integrity that Penney first formalized in 1913 with the "Penney Idea" are still in place today. Pins with the motto, "H.C.S.C." are presented to new management associates in a formal ceremony. An affirmation ceremony is held every four or five years. Its purpose is to welcome partners into the company and reinforce the company's founding principles. According to Howell, the key ingredient in passing on the spirit of integrity is "leadership by example."

How does an organization make certain that integrity permeates the organization? James E. Oesterreicher, Vice Chairman and CEO addresses this problem in these words:

"A company may have an ethics code that prohibits certain business practices, but the prevailing culture may say, 'Do what it takes, just don't let us know about it.' A company can't let down its guard for a moment...unethical behavior can arise at any time within any business."

In other words, it is up to individual leaders to create a high-integrity work environment that allows customers, employees, and the community to meet their needs. Robert Waterman, co-author of *In Search of Excellence,* said in his second book, *The Renewal Factor*, that the effect of any management program pales in comparison to the effect of managers paying attention to the results they want over time. If integrity is the main thing you want in your workplace, leaders must make it important on a daily basis. The same applies to families, civic clubs, churches, schools, and governments. At some level, each of us lead, and we must set the example.

Companies such as JCPenney have the inside track in passing on a heritage of integrity; because generations of managers have worked to keep the principles alive, they are often found posted in the offices of Penney managers. The fact the principles are posted, however, isn't as important as the fact they are practiced. It is the practice of the principles that lead to success.

In a speech given at Texas Christian University in September, 1989, Oesterreicher outlined three additional actions organizations can take to help create a high integrity work environment:

- **Communicate the organization's expectations to employees**
- **Hire and promote based on demonstration of high ethical standards**
- **Deal swiftly with unethical behavior**

For today's leaders at JCPenney, integrity is more than just good business philosophy, it is good business—period. The company continually rates high on customer surveys of honesty, integrity, fair play, and value. They are the fourth largest retailer in North America, with 196,000 full-time associates in 1,300 stores. They operate the nation's second largest catalog business, nearly 500 Thrift Drug stores, and several specialty boutiques. They also own the JCPenney Life Insurance Company and the JCPenney National Bank. Sales in 1989 were more than $16 billion. They have achieved these impressive results by staying true to the mission that existed in 1902, "**To sell merchandise and**

services to customers at a profit in a manner that is consistent with our corporate ethics and responsibilities." In addition to the direct benefits, JCPenney gains some not so obvious advantages:

- They attract people who share their philosophy, so the environment gets perpetuated. They have a great number of second and third generation managers in the company, all of whom have grown up hearing, believing, and living out the Penney philosophy of integrity
- They retain a high percentage of their people. There are many examples of individuals who spend their entire career with this company.
- They attract people who give back to make the community a better place. Most managers are involved in the community. In addition, non-management associates are honored for their contributions to the community. Each year the company confers two awards, The Golden Rule Award and The James Cash Penney Award, to associates and charities who help others.

The JCPenney Company, past and present, provides good corporate and personal role models for integrity. Its success in building integrity as a corporate life style is worth emulating. It is, of course, only one of many examples. Throughout this book we have provided many other specific examples of leaders and organizations who demonstrate their integrity through action. The one common factor we've found in organizations of integrity is that people of intense personal integrity provide leadership-by-example. These leaders share a common commitment to doing the right thing in their relationships with all those with whom they come in contact.

Building High-Integrity Work Environments

JCPenney began building a high integrity work environment in 1902—nine years before publication of the Scout Oath. Its executives are quick to admit that you never arrive at your destination because it is an continuous journey. Management must instill its commitment into each new employee and continually reinforce it with seasoned workers. An old Chinese proverb says, "a journey of a thousand miles begins with a single step." If we are to succeed in building integrity-driven organizations, we must make that beginning. The first step is a commitment by leaders such as you to make integrity a guiding principle for every decision. The second step is to communicate that commitment to your employees, shareholders, customers, suppliers, and the community. That communication is often through the printed and spoken word, but words mean very little unless they are backed by deeds. We can't overstress the importance of performance. If the leadership in any organization is unwilling to practice what it preaches, it would be better off remaining silent.

In our research of successful organizations, we have found high integrity work environments are characterized by the following:

- **Decisions are made on the basis of *what's right* rather than *who's right*.** Which decisions? All decisions. New product design, marketing, business development, employee relations, customer service, sales strategies, accounts payable schedules, contributions to charitable organizations, and everything else that comes up in the organization are subject to one standard—*what is the right thing to do?* We like the standard Carl Sewell uses "How would I feel if my decision was published on the front page of the morning newspaper?"

- **Expectations are clearly communicated.** Employees know what is expected in all areas of their performance, especially in the areas of integrity, quality, and service. The high-integrity organization knows that it is impossible to hold people responsible for something they cannot do or of which they are not aware.

- **Life-long growth, development, and learning are emphasized**. The changing world in which we live requires us to be constantly improving if we are to remain successful. Arie de Geus, retired Coordinator of Group Planning for Royal Dutch/Shell, stated, "The ability to learn faster than our competitors may be the only sustainable competitive advantage." We would add that the high-integrity organization sees continual learning as the minimum required to help customers, employees, and the community meet their needs.

- **There is a high degree of personal commitment.** Commitment is the result of desire mixed with self-discipline. The desire comes from a support for the mission and vision. Self-discipline is the result of learning and practice. Self-disciplined individuals understand their responsibility and perform consistently to meet or exceed those responsibilities. The organization may have to institute a system of accountability to build the structure necessary for some people to learn their responsibilities. Over time, however, the imposed structure will become unnecessary as compliance gives way to self-discipline and commitment.

- **Strong partnerships exist between management and employees, organization and customers, organization and suppliers, and organization and community.** Partnerships are an indicator of trust. We believe trust is the primary result of integrity.

The same criteria, we believe, applies to every organization and not just businesses. Successful families who teach our future leaders about the importance of honor and integrity share these characteristics. So do schools, churches, and entire communities.

Self-Check Your Organization's Integrity Rating

Complete the assessment below to determine your organization's rating as a high-integrity environment. Rate yourself on a scale of 1 to 5 with "5" being *excellent* and "1" being *needs improvement*.

- Decisions are made based on "what's right for all parties" and not on the basis of tradition or political positioning. ____

- People at all levels of the organization clearly understand what is expected of them in areas of productivity, quality, service, job performance, and integrity. ____

- Individuals are continually encouraged to upgrade their technical and relationship-building skills. ____

- Leaders and managers are held accountable for the development of people. ____

- The organization's leaders set a good example of integrity. ____

- Individuals are rewarded for their performance that demonstrates integrity. ____

- The organization deals swiftly with individual performance that violates the trust of others. ____

- The organization has a reputation for honesty, value, and integrity. ____

- Everyone is united behind the common goals of providing quality products and services to customers in a manner that communicates honesty, value, and integrity. ____

- The organization acts responsibly toward the welfare of the community as a whole. ____

SCORING

- If your score is 40 or above, your organization does a terrific job of demonstrating its integrity. There may be a few areas you want to fine tune, but you are doing well.
- If you scored between 30 and 40, you're doing a good job overall, but there are probably a few specific areas on which you should work.
- If your organization scored below 30, you should begin right now to make a specific effort to improve your performance. Your customers and your employees will appreciate your effort, and your organization will become more effective.

The first place to start any improvement effort is with the person you have the most ability to change—yourself. At the end of each chapter we provided you with space to list the things you would do to honor your commitment to the topic covered in the chapter. We would like for you to go back to your commitments at this point and pick the two that are most important from each chapter. When choosing your most important commitments, determine the ones that will have the largest impact on your ability to demonstrate that principle. Then, set specific goals and an action plan to put your commitments into practice. Remember, commitment is demonstrated through action!

The Lure of Expedience

The biggest challenge we face in becoming a leaders of integrity is the lure of expedience. Experience tells us that there are no shortcuts. But, the lure of expedience tempts us to try to gain quick results at the expense of others. The leaders profiled in this book know that long-term success comes only when our commitment to succeed is founded on a solid base of honor and integrity.

Unfortunately, many individuals and organizations talk about integrity while rewarding the lack of it. They focus on short-term profits and encourage a "whatever it takes" approach to achieving them. In this kind of environment, people who would never consider a "major infraction" of the tenets of integrity are presented with peer pressure to betray customers, commitments, confidences, community, and conscience, in order to achieve the goal.

The daily challenges to our sense of honor may appear small on the surface, but our response over time sends the true message about our integrity to those who observe us. Those who observe rightly conclude that if we are willing to sacrifice integrity for the small things, we will probably make the same sacrifice in other areas also. That is why each decision we make is important.

John Delaney and Donna Sockell, associate professors at the Columbia University School of Business, surveyed past graduates to find out their experiences with ethics and integrity. Based on responses from 1,073 individuals, they determined that the average graduate faced 4.2 ethical dilemmas in the past year. The incidents varied from breaking the law to bending corporate policy. The most disturbing portion of their findings was that 40 percent of those who chose to act unethically were rewarded, either explicitly or implicitly, by their organization. An additional 40 percent received no feedback whatsoever from their company, while 31 percent of those who refused to act unethically were implicitly or explicitly punished![2] It is clear that actions speak louder than their words. It does little good to publicly praise integrity if those who exhibit it are punished and those who do not are promoted.

The Ethics Litmus Test

Many years ago, Dr. Harry Emerson Fosdick created a six-point test for deciding right from wrong. Dr. Preston Bradley later adapted the work into what we call the "The Ethics Litmus Test."

1. **Does the course of action you plan to follow seem logical and reasonable? Never mind what anyone else has to say, does it make sense to you? If it does, it is probably right.**
2. **Does it pass the test of sportsmanship? In other words, if everyone followed the same course of action, would the results be beneficial for all?**
3. **Where will your plan of action lead? How will it affect others? What will it do for you?**
4. **Will you think well of yourself when you look back at what you've done?**
5. **Try to separate yourself from the problem. Pretend for a moment it is the problem of the person you most admire. Ask yourself how that person would handle it.**
6. **Hold up the final decision to the glaring light of publicity. Would you want your family and friends to know what you have done? The decisions we make in the hope that no one will find out are usually wrong.**

Building High-Integrity Organizations

Leaders influence the organization in which they operate regardless of their position. However, those in positions of authority face the special challenge of building a cohesive unit that promotes trust internally and externally.

The organizations profiled in this book are rarely mentioned in the media unless the subject is well-run operations with a high sense of integrity. These organizations are the places where people like to work and do business. As we have seen, the first step in building a high-integrity organization is to start with ourselves. There can be no transformation in our business relationships without internal change within us. No internal change without trust. No trust without integrity. But, from that point forward, you will need to encourage the change in your organization. Consider the following to help you complete your task. the language relates to business, but the principles apply anywhere.

1. **Don't announce a new "Integrity Program."** This sounds strange and almost contradictory, but programs historically have both a start and a stop date. Employees often see a program as yet one more example of "management-by-best-seller." In addition, programs have a way of focusing on actions instead of the desired results. Tell people why integrity is important, then prove its importance by the way you reward compliance with policy.

   If you do implement a "program" in the process of building your high integrity organization, make sure everyone knows that the program is only a tool to help you reach a goal. It is important to keep the organization focused on the goal of becoming an organization that personifies integrity. Programs come and go, but values such as integrity, quality, and service are always there as the guiding principles of organizational and personal success.

2. **Decide how you want customers, employees, and customers to perceive your organization.** Communicate your expectations clearly, measure the results, and continue to make integrity important through reinforcement and accountability. There's an old saying that goes, "Results occur when you inspect what you expect." What you expect must not only be inspected, it must be respected—it must be realistic. If your company has a poor reputation among customers or suppliers, don't tell your employees you expect a complete turn-a-round in thirty days. Tell them what your long-term goal is, and set a series of incremental goals that steadily build trust. Once you communicate your reasonable expectations, however, you have a right to expect compliance. Constant measurement, reinforcement, and accountability will send the message that integrity is important—whatever your past track record has been.

3. **Structure your organization's systems to be consistent with your values.** Employees from many organizations have told us that their organization devotes a great deal of time and energy to making sure the customer is treated well while paying little attention to the systems that ensure quality products and services. Smiles and apologies will get you through an occasional lapse, but they won't save you over the long

haul. Long-term success requires systems that ensure things get done right the first time. Each organizational system should be evaluated based on the following questions: Are we doing what we said we would do? Are we providing what we said we would provide?

You need to ask these questions about every organizational system—production, distribution, customer service, financial management, compensation, performance management, selection, marketing, sales, management information systems, engineering, etc. A breakdown in any area will give some the excuse they need to justify their own poor performance. Support the systems with training in areas like communication, decision making, leadership, commitment and responsibility, customer service, quality, and conflict management. You not only need to support these things, you need to promote them.

4. **Promote traditions and legends regarding integrity.** JCPenney recreates the ceremony in which James Cash Penney and the original partners pledged their commitment to the company's values. Mary Kay Cosmetics uses ceremonies to create and promote legends of service, productivity, and integrity. "Foots" Clements gives away marbles inscribed with "The Golden Rule." In other words, make integrity the number one value in your organization, and continually reinforce your commitment.

5. **Remember and practice the three "P's" for managing change—purpose, patience, and persistence.** Change rarely occurs overnight and usually meets with resistance. During the process, it is important to stay focused on the purpose—to develop

an organization that wins the trust of others. Patience and persistence will be necessary, also. Patience with your self, and others, and persistence when you feel like giving up.

As you work to build integrity in your organization, mistakes will be made, some of them yours. Don't become discouraged! An organization free of mistakes is also free of action and learning. When the mistakes are yours, apologize quickly and publicly. When the mistakes are someone else's confront quickly and privately.

What do you do when you meet talented, capable individuals who don't share your commitment to integrity? If that happens, in an organization, it may be necessary for you to remove the individuals from the organization. When this must be done, it is important that it be done properly— remember, the integrity you exercise in this situation will be watched by everyone. In families or personal relationships, the challenges are more difficult. Begin by confronting them with the facts as you know them and listen to their side of the story. Then help them learn from the situation and improve in the future. Change and growth are painful, and there is always the temptation to follow the lure of expedience. There are no shortcuts to integrity— things that appear to be shortcuts are only detours that can lead you in the opposite direction.

What We Found While Writing This Book

Our original idea for this book was to sound a clear clarion-call for a return to traditional values, for our experience in dealing with hundreds of organizations has shown us that for leaders to adhere to Scout-like principles is the only way we can successfully survive the changing times ahead. Peter C. Browning, former Chairman, CEO, and President of National Gypsum Company, summed it up when he told us, "The geographical, political, and economic structures of the twentieth century are undergoing rapid alteration throughout the world. Managing such changes will be the greatest challenge facing American business during the last decade of this century. The ability to attract the right kind of leadership needed for this task will determine in large part, whether we as a nation will be able to compete in this dynamic environment."

Strangely, there are some who want the benefits of honor and integrity without having to actually adhere to those standards themselves. It won't work. It is not enough to acquiesce to the principles mentally—they must be lived.

We feel those who would try to feign honor are in the minority. Among our own clients, we found a high percentage of successful leaders who either had been Boy Scouts or Girl Scouts, or embraced Scout-like ethics and integrity. We contacted them to find the "secret" of their success and each person we interviewed knew or knew of others we should talk to and the list of those we "must interview" kept growing. Every time we mentioned this project, leaders responded with the name of someone we "just had" to speak with. Far too many examples surfaced to include in a book of this length. The stories we selected, then, are merely a "core sample" and not an exhaustive list.

The bottom line is that we have learned that you can behave with honor and integrity and be successful. Not only that, we have evidence from the highest echelons in businesses that behaving like a "Boy Scout" is one of the best ways to become successful.

Hal Johnson, Managing Director in the New York office of Norman Broadbent & Associates, one of the country's most prestigious executive search firms, echoed our belief when he told us that organizations want to know what a job candidate stands for and that he/she can be trusted. Johnson says, "A lack of integrity is often the knock-out punch for candidates who are otherwise very strong."

Roger Staubach, CEO of the Staubach Company, agrees. "I can't think of a better tool for predicting the probability of a person's success in business than a measure of his integrity. If you take pride in who you are, what you do, and who you work for, your value system will be in place and you will succeed."

There will be some who will say that building integrity based on a simple oath and law is too simple. We understand. We are a highly technological society, and we often celebrate complex solutions to complex problems. Yet, it is the simplicity of the thing that makes it so effective. It is simple to memorize and, once committed to memory, it becomes a ready litmus test for integrity that can be applied on the spot in any situation.

We can't guarantee you will be successful if you structure your organization and your life along these principles, but a lot of people have tried it and have been successful. Let's be pragmatic: Any program that has successfully taught **honor, helpfulness, fitness, mental alertness, moral straightness, trustworthiness, loyalty, friendliness, courtesy, kindness, obedience,**

cheerfulness, thrift, bravery, cleanness, and **reverence** to 270 million young men must have something going for it!

We think the time for a revival of traditional standards of honor and integrity is at hand. People from all walks of life are realizing that we are dependent on each other for our mutual success and survival. And, without integrity, the trust that's needed to confront the challenges that lie ahead can never be achieved.

It's difficult to describe how we'll know when this book has done it's job. We could measure sales—that's certainly an indicator, but sales gives us no handle on how many put the principles into practice. We could look for the time when organizations of all sizes operate daily from a foundation of integrity. That's a noble goal, but we're not sure how to measure it. We could look for the time when leaders everywhere start demonstrating their integrity through action. That is certainly presumptuous on our part to believe a single book will have that type of impact. Maybe the best way to know when this book has done its job is if someone calls a person of integrity a "real Boy Scout" or a "Girl Scout" they mean it for what it is: a sincere compliment and a sign of respect and admiration. In his book, *Presidential Anecdotes,*[3] Paul F. Boller states that President Gerald R. Ford, "was 'Mr. Nice Guy.' He was, someone said, a 'Boy Scout in the White House.' Boller went on to quote Michigan Senator Robert P. Griffin as saying, "The nicest thing about Jerry Ford, is that he just doesn't have enemies." Boller added, "Even Congressman Paul McCloskey of California, who opposed Ford on vital issues, thought well of him. 'I get tears in my eyes,' he said, 'when I think about Jerry Ford. We love him.' "

That's the kind of reaction you'll get when you operate like a "real Boy Scout" and work and live with Scout-like integrity!

There will always be detractors, those who laugh at honor and integrity and the traditional values that built our great country, our great companies, and our great organizations. They will say that these principles do not fit in our rapidly changing world. But we wouldn't want to be led by them—would you?

CHAPTER NOTES

Chapter 1

[1] Not his real name.

[2] Not his name or position.

[3] Proverbs 23:7.

[4] The term "we" from this point forward in the text refers to the authors unless otherwise indicated.

Chapter 2

[1] *Walking With God* (Abingdon Press, 1928).

[2] *Webster's New Collegiate Dictionary* (G. & C. Merriam Company, 1975).

[3] Noah Webster, *An American Dictionary of the English Language*, 1828.

[4] Frank Luksa, columnist, "As always, Danny White has cross words for strike," *The Dallas Morning News*, March 3, 1995.

[5] Improvements in manufacturing processes had increased production at the mill by 60 percent and Carnegie had 218 workers who were under contract to be paid so much per ton of steel produced. When the contract was up, the company asked that they split the difference and the workers take a 30 percent wage hike as the 60 percent increase in tonnage was due to the new process, not the workers themselves. The union refused the offer and a bitter strike followed.

[6] *The Autobiography of Andrew Carnegie* (Houghton Mifflin, 1920).

Chapter 3

[1] *The Prevention and Collection of Problem Loans* (Bank Administration Institute, 1989), *Selling Strategies for Today's Bankers: A Survival Guide for Tomorrow* (Dearborn Press, 1990).

[2] Sam Walton with John Huey, *Sam Walton: Made In America* (Bantam Books, 1993) 4.

[3] Ibid, 23.

[4] Ibid, 11.

Chapter 4

[1] Marc Bockmon, *Turning Points: The National Gypsum Story* (Taylor Publishing, 1990).

[2] John Bartlett, *Bartlett's Familiar Quotations*, Fifteenth and 125th Anniversary Edition (Little Brown and Company, 1980) 275.19. There is some controversy over the exact translation of Corneille's quote. Oxford quotations translates it as "Do your Duty and leave the issue to the Gods." Either way, the challenge of successful leadership is to do one's duty, regardless of the short term costs.

[3] Stephen E. Ambrose, *Eisenhower: Soldier and President* (Touchstone, 1991), 15-16.

[4] *Character and Leadership* lecture series sponsored by the Lyndon B. Johnson School of Public Affairs the University of Texas carried by C-SPAN.

[5] Stephen E. Ambrose, *Eisenhower: Soldier and President* (Touchstone, 1991), 248.

Chapter 5
[1] Paraphrased from Luke 6:31.
[2] Genesis 4:9.

Chapter 6
[1] Ralph Waldo Emerson, "Letters and Social Aims," 1875.
[2] Proverbs 17:22.
[3] Max DePree, *Leadership Is An Art* (Doubleday, 1989), 7.
[4] Ibid, 9.
[5] Ibid, xiv.
[6] In 1915, health insurance was called "sickness insurance."
[7] Reference from a secondary source, James C. Collins & Jerry I. Porras, *Built To Last: Successful Habits of Visionary Companies* (Harper Business, 1994).
[8] Fred "Chico" Lager, *Ben & Jerry's: The Inside Scoop* (Crown, 19940), 177.
[9] Ibid, 214.
[10] Benjamin Franklin, *The Autobiography and Other Writings*.

Chapter 7
[1] Luke 22:25. " …but he that is greatest among you, let him be as chief, as he that doth serve."
[2] MacMillian Publishing Company, 1987.
[3] Berkley, 1987.
[4] William Morrow and Company, 1982.

[5] Ken Shelton, Editor, "Ten Million Chances to Excel", *Empowering Business Resources*: *Executive Excellence on Productivity* (Scott Foresman and Company, 1990).

[6] Personal interview with Randy Pennington.

[7] Doubleday/Currency, 1990.

Chapter 8

[1] Bernie S. Siegel, M.D. practices surgery in New Haven, CT and teaches at Yale University. His book *Love, Medicine and Miracles* (Harper and Row Publishers, Inc., 1986) shares many examples and techniques for maximizing our self-healing capabilities.

[2] Bantam Books, 1980.

[3] Ken Shelton, Editor, *Empowering Business Resources: Executive Excellence on Productivity* (Scott, Foresman and Company, 1990).

[4] Ibid.

[5] Fleming H. Revell Company, 1971.

[6] Simon and Schuster, 1989. 101.

Chapter 9

[1] Song 2:15.

[2] *Training*, September 1990. 14-15.

[3] Penguin Books, 1981.

About the Authors

Randy Pennington is a sought after speaker, workshop leader and consultant. He regularly works with organizations and their people in the areas of leadership development, becoming integrity-driven, building commitment to results & relationships, and managing change. For more information, please contact:

> **Pennington Performance Group**
> **4000 Winter Park Lane**
> **Dallas, TX 75244**
> **214-980-9857 or 800-779-5295**

Marc Bockmon is a business communicator and writer. He has worked with over three hundred organizations in helping them effectively communicating their ideas. For more information, please contact:

> **Mark Bockmon, President**
> **Experts Unlimited, Ltd.**
> **P. O. Box 3000-2403**
> **Georgetown, TX 78628**
> **512-869-0447**

ADDITIONAL PRODUCTS AND SERVICES

Pennington Performance Group offers a variety of products, services and educational programs to help organizations and their people develop leaders, build trust and become integrity-driven. Resources from the Pennington Performance Group have been used by individuals, businesses, non-profit associations and government agencies. They include:

- On My Honor, I Will Discussion Guide (available Fall 1995)
- On My Honor, I Will Personal Development Workshop
- INTEGRITY-DRIVEN™ Leadership Workshop
- INTEGRITY-DRIVEN™ Leadership 360° Feedback Process
- TOTAL PERFORMANCE™ Management System
- Putting Ethics Into Practice Workshop
- Putting Ethics Into Practice Train-the-Trainer Certification
- Managing for Results & Relationships Workshop and 360° Feedback Process
- Custom consulting strategies to
  - help organizations become integrity driven
  - help communities and non-profit groups develop a long-term vision
  - help municipal governments develop strategies, structures and systems to improve the quality of life

- Custom educational sessions and speeches on the following topics:
    - INTEGRITY-DRIVEN™ Leadership
    - Rethinking the Path to Success: Using the Honor Principle to Achieve Success
    - Values Based Decision Making
    - Reinventing the Organization to Cooperate & Compete
    - Meeting the Challenges of Change
    - Managing for Results & Relationships

For additional information or to be notified of future product and service developments, please contact:
Pennington Performance Group
4000 Winter Park Lane
Dallas, TX 75244
214-980-9857

Experts Unlimited offers professional creative services for sales and training films, seminars and meetings. They are a leading edge creator of interactive, computer based training.

For additional information please contact:
Experts Unlimited, Ltd.
P. O. Box 3000-2403
Georgetown, Texas 78628
512-869-0447